ROGER L. STEVENS PRESENTS

ROGER L. STEVENS PRESENTS

ESSAYS BY *E. J. Kahn, Jr.*
Walter Zvonchenko
Ruth Mayleas
Tom Prideaux
David Richards

LIBRARY OF CONGRESS   WASHINGTON   2002

Director of Publishing: W. Ralph Eubanks
Editor: Iris Newsom
Designer: Stephen Kraft

This book, and the accompanying exhibition, were made possible through the generosity of Christine Stevens and her daughter, Christabel Stevens Gough.

∞ The paper used in this publication meets the requirements for permanence established by the American National Standard for Information Services "Permanence of Paper for Printed Library Materials" (ANSI Z39.48-1984.)

Library of Congress Cataloging-in-Publication Data

Roger L. Stevens presents: essays by E. J. Kahn . . . [et al.]
   p. cm.
Contents: Introduction/James H. Billington—Profiles, openings and closings / E. J. Kahn, Jr.—Roger L. Stevens on Broadway and in the West End / Walter Zvonchenko—Roger Stevens, the arts endowment years—The Theatre Program years / Ruth Mayleas—The man behind Washington's Kennedy Center/Tom Prideaux—Roger Stevens, an appreciation / David Richards / Overview of the Roger L. Stevens collection—Roger L. Stevens's productions 1947–1987.
ISBN 0-8444-1053-5
1. Stevens, Roger L.—Exhibitions. I. Kahn, E. J. (Ely Jacques), 1916-
PN2287.S6785 R64 2002
792'.0232'092–dc21   2001050526

Cover: Roger Stevens standing on West 45th Street, in the New York theatre district.

Frontispiece: Interior of New York's Empire Theatre. Demolished in 1953, this much-loved theatre was home to Roger Stevens's first presentation in New York, a production of Shakespeare's *Twelfth Night*, which opened on October 3, 1949. In *Lost Broadway Theatres*, by William van Hoogstraten. *General Collections, Library of Congress.*

Contents

James H. Billington, Librarian of Congress	Introduction **6**
E. J. Kahn, Jr.	Profiles: Openings and Closings **8**
Walter Zvonchenko	Roger L. Stevens on Broadway and in the West End **40**
Ruth Mayleas	Roger Stevens: The Arts Endowment Years—The Theatre Program **66**
Tom Prideaux	The Man Behind Washington's Kennedy Center **79**
David Richards	Roger Stevens: An Appreciation **96**
	Overview of the Roger L. Stevens Collection **118**
	Roger L. Stevens's Productions 1949-1987 **120**
	Contributors **134**

Introduction

Roger L. Stevens's career was characterized by an intense love of the theatre and the pursuit of excellence. I was one of many to benefit from his efforts long before I knew him.

As a student in the late 1940s, I saw a production of a play by Jean Giraudoux, one of the best-regarded writers for the French stage in the early twentieth century. An adaptation of his *The Madwoman of Chaillot*, with Martita Hunt playing one of the three eccentric and elderly Parisian ladies who fight and win an extremely unorthodox battle against evil in the world, had received substantial financial support from a Detroit real estate agent, Roger L. Stevens. I was exhilarated by this early example of the level of quality that would become associated with this man who subsequently had such a strong impact on the nation's cultural life in the second half of the century.

The generosity of Roger and Christine Stevens has brought to the Library the Stevens papers, which encompass decades of American cultural life and testify to the extent of Stevens's interests and projects. A glance through the collection's finding aid reveals a wide range of activities. A deeper inquiry into the papers themselves shows far-reaching results.

The Library's exhibition and this book, *Roger L. Stevens Presents*, document Stevens's life and career and his efforts to raise the level of the performing arts in the nation. Many of his high-quality American and European stage productions were clearly not going to be financially profitable; but if Stevens believed in their worth, he supported them and gave us the opportunity to experience them.

Stevens had a talent for identifying the critical elements and personalities in any situation, whether in real estate or cultural affairs. If one organizational structure could be combined successfully with another, no matter how apparently disparate in character or aim, he seized the opportunity. His personal calendars attest to the variety of concerns that demanded his daily attention and helped him develop new plans and projects.

During the 1950s, as his careers in theatre and real estate grew and prospered, Stevens began exerting an influence on the nation's educational and artistic institutions. His papers include files on his activities as a member of the board of the Metropolitan Opera and Ballet Theatre, and as a trustee of the American Shakespeare Theatre and many others.

Stevens's capacity for reaching toward ever-new horizons prompted Pres. John F. Kennedy to appoint him to head the project to build Washington's National Cultural Center. This project, which ultimately became the John F. Kennedy Center for the Performing Arts, demanded a leader with artistic vision and expertise in both stage administration and land development. Stevens had the perfect background.

After the death of President Kennedy, when Stevens was moving ahead with the early stages of developing the Kennedy Center, Pres. Lyndon B. Johnson appointed him head of the National Council on the Arts and then first chairman of the National Endowment for the Arts. Beginning with very little funding, Stevens put together an organization that gave promise early on of becoming a powerful force for the expansion and enrichment of our cultural life.

Roger Stevens not only built a world-class performance center in the nation's capital, he inspired us all with his unquenchable enthusiasm for, and support of, the arts. His career and accomplishments would have qualified him to be appointed as the nation's first Secretary of Cultural Affairs, had such a position existed. But Roger Stevens did not need a title to leave a legacy. He worked ceaselessly, even late in his life when he was ill, to bring the magic of the theatre into all our lives.

James H. Billington
Librarian of Congress

Profiles:
Closings and Openings–I

E.J. Kahn, Jr.

During the last couple of years, no individual has had a bigger impact on the American real-estate scene than a man who organized and headed a syndicate that bought, for fifty-one and a half million dollars, the Empire State Building; who, by agreeing to pay rent that, over a thirty-five-year stretch, will probably come to more than fifty million dollars, acquired the much-coveted lease on a ten-acre slice of downtown Seattle; and who is at present planning the construction in Boston of a seventy-five-million-dollar commercial center which, if it materializes, will be more than twice as spacious as the Rockefellers' center here. During the same period, no individual has had a bigger impact on the legitimate theatre than a man who is currently its busiest producer and has been instrumental, this season alone, in bringing to Broadway "Tea and Sympathy," "Sabrina Fair," "In the Summer House," "The Remarkable Mr. Pennypacker," and "Escapade"; who has "The Confidential Clerk," "The Winner," and "Ondine" coming up any day now; and whose agenda for next season includes the importation from Stratford-on-Avon of the Shakespeare Memorial Theatre Company. The fact that the individual in both instances is the same man is a source of wonder to his associates and of occasional concern to the man himself—Roger Lacey Stevens, a forty-three-year-old entrepreneur from Michigan with a vast enthusiasm for both second acts and second mortgages. Stevens, a tall, powerfully built, bald-headed, affable plunger, cannot make up his mind which aspect of his dual personality is dominant, and in introspective moments he is apt to try to analyze himself after the manner of his favorite playwright, Luigi Pirandello, who was obsessed with the complexity of human nature and with man's inability to fathom his own true identity. Not long ago, discussing his double-barrelled existence with a friend, Stevens paused suddenly, like a character in a play, and asked, "Who am I?"

Even those who are closest to Stevens aren't sure who he is—or, rather, what be is—and people who have seen a good deal of him in one of his occupational roles have been astonished, and sometimes put out, to learn that there is another side to him. Once, a theatrical director who was anxious to confer with him about a leading lady was miffed on being told that he was inextricably tied up in a conference with J. P. Morgan & Co. about a multimillion-dollar loan for an imminent building venture. "How can anybody bother with a hole in the

Reprinted by permission; © 1954 E. J. Kahn, Jr.
Originally published in *The New Yorker* (February 13 and 20, 1954). All rights reserved.

Jean Giraudoux's *The Madwoman of Chaillot,* as adapted by Maurice Valency, opened in New York at the Belasco Theatre on December 27, 1948, with (right to left) Estelle Winwood, Martita Hunt, and Nydia Westman. One of the major investors in the production was Roger L. Stevens at a time just before he became a theatrical producer on Broadway. *Van Damm Photographs, Music Division, Library of Congress.*

ground when we're *casting!*" the director exclaimed. More recently, a young Boston architect who has been working on Stevens' center there was dismayed when he found out that Stevens, whom he had thought of as a man interested exclusively in such matters as floor space and elevators, was the impresario of a number of Broadway plays that had been tried out in Boston, "It came as a kind of shock to discover that all this time Deborah Kerr and I have been working for the same boss," he said.

In both his chosen spheres of activity, Stevens has a chameleon's faculty for making himself inconspicuous. Though he has been chairman of the executive committee of the Empire State Building, for over two years, he is not known by sight to the guards of the observation tower. Similarly, he is now and then flagged down by stage doormen while he is on his way to visit the dressing rooms of actors in his employ. Stevens was not surprised at the treatment he received in an article that *Theatre Arts* carried last November outlining the steps that led to the New York opening of "'Tea and Sympathy," which was produced by the Playwrights' Company in association with Mrs. Mary K. Frank. While Stevens has never written a play, he has been a member of the Playwrights since 1951, and he was more responsible than any playwriting Playwright for bringing "Tea and Sympathy" to Broadway. *Theatre Arts* accompanied its article with photographs of practically all the people connected with the production—director, actors, playwright, costume designer, wardrobe mistress, scene designer, stage hands, and so on. The only face of consequence missing was that of Stevens, whose name, however, appeared under a picture of the company manager. Stevens seems to enjoy being cast in the role of a naive country bumpkin turned loose to wander unrecognized through the big city—a faceless lamb, as it were, thrown among celebrated lions. A few weeks ago, as he was escorting a friend to one of his shows, he said, "It's almost curtain time. I sure hope they'll hold my tickets for me."

Some of Stevens' acquaintances believe that he is given to overacting his lamb-among-lions role. They point out that he has become sufficiently polished to be warmly greeted by, and to confidently order a bottle of wine from, such a connoisseur of urbanity as the headwaiter of the Baroque, and that not long ago, when a Wall Street friend put him up for the Racquet and Tennis Club, he did not hesitate to join it. In fact, these acquaintances suggest that Stevens' habitual air of naivete is a carefully contrived suit of armor that he finds useful in dickering with people who both appear and are tough. After tangling with an outwardly diffident Stevens in one mammoth real-estate operation, an executive of the Prudential Insurance Company, whose negotiations must by the nature of their work be masters of the firm stand, was moved to remark admiringly that the man had ice water in his veins.

Whatever the contents of Stevens' veins, it was definitely a warm-hearted impulse that led him into the real-estate deal–one of the biggest ever brought off west of the Mississippi–that resulted in his now being the operator of a highly profitable cluster of structures in Seattle that includes six large office buildings and the city's principal movie house. Stevens got mixed up in this one as the outcome of paying a casual call on a man who was employed in Detroit by an insurance company to look after its real-estate holdings. While the insurance man was on the phone, Stevens idly examined a pile of magazines on his desk. Stevens is a man with a predilection for plays that he thinks have real literary merit rather than mere popular appeal, and since he feels the same way about books and magazines, he was delighted to find, tucked away beneath *Collier's* and the *Reader's Digest,* copies of such favorites of his as the *New Republic* and the *Saturday Review.* He was also amazed. "I didn't know anybody in the financial world read those things except me," he said later. As soon as his companion had put down the phone, Stevens struck up a lively intellectual conversation with him—the sort of conversation he had never before enjoyed in an insurance office. As Stevens was about to leave, the insurance man remarked that he wanted very much to return to Seattle, where he had been born, but didn't dare give up his job and go because he wasn't sure he could get a comparable one there. Stevens, distressed at finding so mentally stimulating a compan-

Roger Stevens's purchase of the Empire State Building in 1951 became a matter of national attention. It was the tallest structure in the world at the time and a major American monument. An extraordinary number of people participated in the final closing. *Life*, January 7, 1952. *General Collections, Library of Congress.*

ion dissatisfied with his lot, at once invited the man to work for him, at double the salary he was earning, and gave him an ideal assignment. The University of Washington, which had been bequeathed a substantial portion of the Seattle business district many years before, was looking for a new lessee for the property. Stevens, who had never been in the State of Washington and had no particular desire to go there, instructed his new employee to make a bid to take over the lease. It was Stevens' idea that if things worked out right, he would make the man his resident agent in Seattle. Things were working out fine when, on the day before the contract was to be signed, the man died of a heart attack. Stevens, whose designs on the Far West had been motivated mostly by sentiment, now found himself heavily committed in that remote and unfamiliar territory, and without the benefit of a home-town boy's guidance. Pulling himself together, he boarded a plane for Seattle, and signed the contract. His investment has been doing very nicely.

When Stevens was in his late teens, he kept himself in pocket money by consistently winning small sums from contemporaries who were less skilled than he was at bridge, black-jack, and poker. He no longer plays cards much, but in times of stress he often adopts the disconcertingly phlegmatic attitude of an experienced gambler, which, of course, is essentially what he is—the high-class variety of gambler known as a speculator. Before he succeeded in nailing down the Empire State Building, he wagered a million-dollar cash deposit—a large part of it belonging to associates who were, in effect, betting on his ability to bring off the deal—on the proposition that he could raise an additional fifty and a half million within a specified time; if he had failed to come through he would have had to forfeit the ante. Stevens beat the deadline, but only by forty-eight hours—a margin of safety that many poker players, considering the stakes, might think inadequate. In taking the chances he does, Stevens, like most other big-time dealers in real estate today, rarely uses much of his own money. He prefers to borrow—or, as he puts it, to hire—money from banks, insurance companies, or any other sources that he can tap. "The funny thing about what I do is that if I had the money myself, I wouldn't do it," he says. "The romance of speculation lies in doing it with little money of your own." When the Empire State Building finally changed hands, Stevens personally owned a two-million-dollar slice of it, for which he had invested a mere eight hundred thousand dollars–two hundred and fifty thousand of them being the broker's commission he collected on the sale.

Among the real-estate men, the gathering of so lush a harvest from so relatively puny a planting is considered not unreasonable; they look upon it as a legitimate reward for having the courage, imagination, and ability to conceive a big transaction and see it through to completion. Since it was Stevens who painstakingly fitted together the myriad bits and pieces that made up the Empire State transaction, and who, irrespective of the amount of cash he put up personally, staked his whole reputation on having the deal pan out, these men feel that it was only right that he should have something substantial to show for it. "Somebody has to take chances to get things done under our economic system," a friend of Stevens' observed recently. "A lot of people won't take them. But Roger will, and, what's more, he has the gift of persuading hardheaded businessmen to go along with him. He's a natural coordinator. He's also the most natural money-maker I've ever met. Sometimes, with all the projects he's embroiled in now, people think he's a stretched-out man—a guy who's so overextended that a depression would really clip him. But you can't talk to Roger about depressions. It would be like talking to a race horse about running slower. Men like Roger are running to win. I If they stopped to think about all the awful things that could happen to them, they wouldn't win. Speculation is a matter of intuition rather than intelligence, anyway. With Roger, the closing's the thing, and he doesn't go into a deal unless he has a strong hunch he can close it. It's true that he made a big profit on the Empire State deal, but he made a bigger gamble. What he did basically was push in his entire stack of chips. But he won the pot when he closed. And he's never missed out on a closing yet."

Stevens has scarcely missed out on an opening, either, since he became stage-struck. A few years ago, his wife was out of town on the opening of a play he owned a piece of, and he chivalrously waited to go to it with her. She arrived in New York two days later, expecting to see the show with her husband that evening, but by then it had folded. Having failed to catch that particular turkey made Stevens resolve never again to miss an opening if he could help it, whether or not he had a financial interest in the show. Stevens got into the theatre shortly after the Second World War, when, after being mustered out of the Navy, he decided that the majority of the real-estate people he associated with were culturally sterile and severely limited in conversational scope. (He had not yet met the man from Seattle.) They could talk only shop. Stevens found this boring, at least after business hours, when he would rather discuss arts than crafts. He was then living in Ann Arbor, but he visited New York frequently and went to plays as often as possible. He began to get better acquainted with the theatre by investing comparatively small amounts in a few plays, and he has been an angel ever since. His wingspread has never been as ample as, say, Howard Cullman's, but he has backed quite a few shows—mostly off-beat, unconventional ones of a ruggedly serious nature. Among them have been "The Madwoman of Chaillot," "Saint Joan," "Venus Observed," "Second Threshold," "Legend of Lovers," "Darkness at Noon," "Not for Children," "Barefoot in Athens," "An Enemy of the People," "The Rose Tattoo," "Camino Real," and "Peer Gynt." In backing shows and, for the past five years, producing them as well, he has spent a lot of money on the theatre, but he has not spent it primarily in the hope of financial reward and therefore regards his Broadway operations as not truly speculative. "Most shows are lousy investments unless you have a good tax base and don't mind losing money," he says.

At the start of his career as an angel, Stevens, always a persuasive salesman, induced several of his real-estate partners to join him in backing plays; they were men whose tax bases were in such excellent shape that he didn't mind asking them to invest in things like Ibsen, even though he may have doubted their ability to discourse upon them. A few of these associates have stuck with him in his theatrical adventures ever since, through thick and a good deal of thin. "I have managed to avoid hits assiduously," Stevens said at the beginning of the present season. This gloomy claim was not entirely true at the time, for he had acquired on behalf of the Playwrights' Company the production rights to "The Fourposter," as the result of losing his way while driving to see a summer-theatre tryout of the show on Cape Cod. He didn't arrive until the last act was half finished. He stayed over an extra day so he could take in the whole play, and, rather than waste his time just hanging around, spent the interval negotiating for the Broadway rights.

Stevens has run into some exasperating difficulties trying to cut his real-estate friends in on hits he hasn't managed to avoid. He was preoccupied with real-estate matters at the time the Playwrights began to dispose of shares of "The Fourposter," and these went so fast that when he got around to trying to fix his friends up he was able to wangle only a piddling portion of it for them. In the case of "Tea and Sympathy," he fared even worse. Last spring, shortly before he was to sail for Europe, he was weighing the merits of three scripts, one of them "Tea and Sympathy," when he ran into Mrs. Frank, who informed him that she had a lot of money lined up to produce a show with, but no show. "I'm long on scripts but short on time to raise money," Stevens told her, and, in the name of his fellow Playwrights, solved the double dilemma by selling Mrs. Frank half of "Tea and Sympathy." A month later, upon returning to New York, he learned that Deborah Kerr had been signed for the play, that it looked exceedingly promising, and that all the money needed to produce it had been subscribed. The following day, two real-estate men who had gamely gone along with Stevens through a number of tooth-rattling fiascoes called on him to inquire eagerly how much of "Tea and Sympathy" he had saved for them. "Oh, you wouldn't like it," Stevens said uncomfortably. "It's very arty." They declared that they were sure they would like it, and that in artiness they didn't believe it could approach either "Legend of Lovers" or "An Enemy of the People," the sour memories of which were still making their jaws ache. Stevens sighed, and stoically gave up most of his own share of the show to his friends.

Stevens took his first step up the ladder from angel to producer in the spring of 1949, when he put on "Twelfth Night," with a cast of imported Broadway actors, at the Ann Arbor Drama Festival. That fall, he moved in on New York as a real-estate operator and brought "Twelfth Night" along, with most of its original cast. In making the jump to the big time, Stevens was encouraged by Michael Myerberg, an experienced Broadway producer, who told him, "There's no better way to start than with Shakespeare," Stevens was further encouraged when Brooks Atkinson gave "Twelfth Night" an approving notice. That was about all the encouragement he got, but for him it was enough; in the face of massive public apathy, he kept the show running until he had lost forty-five thousand dollars on it. In the spring of 1950, Stevens became a member of the board of directors of the American National Theatre and Academy, or ANTA. He gave ANTA twenty-five thousand dollars to underwrite the production of a series of plays, and an additional twenty-five thousand to make up the difference between what it finally cost to produce one of them, "Peer Gynt," and the show's budget. When ANTA rejected his suggestion that it put on "Peter Pan," he produced the play with Peter Lawrence, who owned the rights to It. This was a hit, but its expenses were so high that, although it ran for forty weeks at an operating profit, it fell short by fifty-eight thousand dollars, a good many of them Stevens', of earning back its production costs.

As his next step up the ladder, Stevens became a member of the Playwrights' Company, which had been founded in 1938 by Maxwell Anderson, S. N. Behrman, Sidney Howard, Elmer Rice, and Robert E. Sherwood. The idea was that they would produce their own works. Howard died and Behrman dropped out. At the start of 1951 there were four members—the three remaining playwrights and John F. Wharton, a theatrical lawyer who was representing Stevens in his stage transactions. It was through Wharton that Stevens was invited to join the Playwrights. (Its membership has since risen to six, Robert Anderson, a bonafide playwright and the author of "Tea and Sympathy," having joined it last October.)

Stevens' functions were to dig up promising plays, since Maxwell

Roger Stevens joined the Playwrights' Company in 1951. He is seen here with Elmer Rice, John Wharton, Maxwell Anderson, and Robert Sherwood, who were among the founding members of the company, which was organized to promote the production of the members' plays. *Roger L. Stevens Collection, Music Division, Library of Congress.*

Caricature of Robert Sherwood by Covarrubias. One of the founding members of the Playwrights' Company, Sherwood, in addition to working on his own plays, frequently took a major role in fostering the production of other plays, including *The Fourposter* and *Ondine*, which were done during Stevens's association with the Company. *Prints and Photographs Division, Library of Congress.*

Jessica Tandy and Hume Cronyn in *The Fourposter*, a play which Stevens fostered for production by the Playwrights' Company. With direction by Jose Ferrer, it was a great success, both critically and financially. World Telegram and Sun *Collection, Prints and Photographs Division, Library of Congress.*

Anderson, Rice, and Sherwood couldn't write enough to keep the group occupied, and, even more important, to raise money. The Playwrights were impressed by his golden touch, as well they might have been. Some producers have to scramble for backing; Stevens has been known to scratch up ten thousand dollars, in small amounts, merely by fitting a series of strategically placed phone calls into an already crowded morning. Calling a businessman in Chicago, perhaps, or Cleveland–both are cities in which he has at one time or another owned large chunks of real estate–he will say in an offhand way, "I was just wondering how your money was holding out. I seem to have a couple of new plays coming up here. I don't want to be accused of leaving you out, you know." And that will just about be that.

Roger Stevens standing on West 45th Street, one of the busiest theatre streets in New York's Times Square area, and home to a great many stage productions with which Stevens was associated. *Roger L. Stevens Collection, Music Division, Library of Congress.*

Lately, Stevens has been the principal driving force behind the establishment of a new theatrical organization, which *Variety* believes may conceivably rival the Shuberts' someday and in which Stevens plays enough roles to make a piker of Ruth Draper. Shortly after he came to New York, he became well acquainted with another stage-minded real-estate man—Robert W. Dowling, the chairman of the board of ANTA and the president of the City Investing Company, of which Stevens is now a director and which owns the Carlyle Hotel, where Stevens has an apartment. Through ANTA, Stevens got to know Robert Whitehead, who was helping direct its play series and was a producer on his own besides. With these two new friends, Stevens presently pieced together a theatrical deal as splendid in its ramifications as any real-estate deal he has concocted. The focal point of this one is the Producers' Theatre (president and treasurer: Stevens), a million-dollar corporation, fifty per cent of which is owned by a corporation known as Whitehead-Stevens Productions (vice-president: Stevens) and fifty per cent by the City Investing Company (director and tenant: Stevens). Of the Whitehead-Stevens share, fourteen per cent is owned by the Playwrights' Company (member: Stevens). Except for City Investing, all these groups–as well as ANTA (director and patron: Stevens)—have set up a joint headquarters in a suite of offices in the Gayety Theatre Building, where, since there is only one Stevens, they are not as pressed for space as they might otherwise be. According to present plans, the Producers' Theatre, whose first production was "The Remarkable Mr. Pennypacker," will operate on a practically non-stop, year-round basis, and its organizers have already obtained ten-year leases on three theatres—the Fulton, the Morosco, and the Coronet—whose lights they hope to keep constantly ablaze. The leases were not very hard to get, since these theatres are owned by City Playhouses, a subsidiary of the City Investing Company. While the Playwrights will continue to produce independently of the Producers' Theatre whenever they feel like it, Whitehead-Stevens will guarantee the Playwrights a substantial amount of financial backing for all their shows. "And to think that less than five years ago Roger was monkeying around with drama festivals in Michigan!" a bewildered friend of the kingpin in this theatrical colossus said recently.

Since the theatre is never a placid institution, a producer with just one burgeoning show on his hands is apt to feel as if he were on the verge of bedlam. Early this season, Stevens suddenly turned to a companion and said, "I must be a madman. I am directly involved at this instant in the production of eight shows." One of the reasons he survives in his self-made maelstrom is that he has a talent for simplification. Among his eight shows was "In the Summer House," which would have been ready to be put on right then if it had had a leading lady. Several people associated with Stevens thought—as did he—that Judith Anderson, who was then at liberty in New York, and had read the script, would be ideal, and, in the customary roundabout manner of doing things in the theatre, they began to devise ingenious ways of, as the saying goes, getting to her. One man suggested to Stevens that if he called up Joshua Logan, who was then out West, he might be able to persuade Logan to telephone Miss Anderson in New York and say a good word for the play. A second counsellor proposed that Stevens urge Elia Kazan to try to get to her, and a third plumped for José Ferrer. Various other important stage names were dropped, and even flung, while Stevens listened respectfully. Then he picked up a phone, called Miss Anderson, and, after a minute or two of polite chitchat, said, "You've been looking for a play for quite a while. Why don't we sit down and make a deal?" A few days later, she signed a contract.

Another of Stevens' eight shows was "Escapade." When he decided that he wanted the American rights to this play, which has to do with

Marianne Moore, one of the great poets of the twentieth century, with Roger Stevens and Roger W. Straus, Jr., president of the publishing house Farrar, Straus, and Giroux. Stevens was active in a great number of cultural institutions, among them the National Book Foundation. Moore was given the Foundation's National Book Award for poetry in 1952. *Roger L. Stevens Collection, Music Division, Library of Congress.*

the vexations of a husband and wife who have three boys in boarding school, he simply put in a transatlantic call to Henry Sherek, who had produced it in England, and picked up the rights over the phone. Stevens thought he was buying the play for the Playwrights to produce under an agreement he had worked out with the other members of the group. Until he joined their ranks, it was their custom to put on only shows of which all the members approved, but Stevens considered this policy impractical; he contended that it was a waste of time and trouble, and that too many desirable scripts might be grabbed up by rival producers while one laggard Playwright was nodding over his homework. He finally prevailed on his colleagues to accept his unseconded appraisal of scripts, with one qualification: He promised to submit to them any play he wanted to buy that touched on politically controversial themes. When he bought "Escapade," he thought from what he had heard about it that it was not politically controversial, but after the script arrived and he had had a chance to read it he got cold feet, so to be on the safe side he showed it to Robert Sherwood, the only other Playwright who happened to be around. Sherwood glanced through it hastily and decided that it was politically innocuous; then he read it carefully as a play, and groaned. In view of this reaction, Stevens decided there was nothing to be gained by asserting his right to produce the play as a Playwrights venture and, instead, took it to his Producers' Theatre partners, Robert Dowling and Robert Whitehead. Both read it and groaned. Shaken but undaunted, Stevens there-

Scott McKay, Cathleen Nesbitt, Robert Duke, Joseph Cotten, and Margaret Sullavan in *Sabrina Fair*, produced by the Playwrights' Company. Samuel Taylor's successful comedy opened in New York on November 11, 1953. World Telegram and Sun *Collection, Prints and Photographs Division, Library of Congress.*

upon bypassed the Producers' Theatre, too, and put the show on in collaboration with Alfred de Liagre, Jr., who was one of Stevens' first theatrical acquaintances and who also liked the play. "I toyed with the idea of advertising it with the line 'If your name's Bob, don't come to this play,'" Stevens says. As it turned out, not many people named Bob or anything else came to the play, and it fizzled after thirteen performances.

Stevens, unlike many of the New York drama critics, admires contemporary English plays. "Anybody interested in the theatre gravitates to London as a hungry man gravitates to a meal," he says. Indeed he is so irresistibly drawn to the stage in London (where the newspapers, impressed with his Empire State Building connections, refer to him as the Skyscraper King) that he has produced a play there, too–with indifferent success. This was early in 1952, and the play was "The Trial of Mr. Pickwick," based on the "Pickwick Papers." He later brought it, austerely retitled "Mr. Pickwick," to this country, where it was a flop. Stevens makes at least one pilgrimage a year to England; on a recent trip he stayed twenty-five days and saw twenty-five shows including a production of "Coriolanus," by the Shakespeare company at Stratford-on-Avon, which he attended with Sherek. After the performance, Stevens asked, more or less rhetorically, "Why doesn't somebody bring this outfit over to the States?" "Why don't you?" Sherek replied. The next thing Stevens knew, he was committed to bringing it over this coming November. He has since recruited his associates in the Producers' Theatre and the Playwrights' Company as co-sponsors. "What pleases me about the idea of having the Stratford company here," Stevens remarked not long ago, "is that after all these years I'm finally going to get to see a production of Shakespeare in this country in which I can understand more than two thirds of what's being said."

Nowadays, when reflecting on his early life, Stevens sometimes gives the impression that his story is in the American tradition of the penniless boy who becomes a successful graduate of the school of hard knocks, and he is fond of saying that during the early thirties he was often without streetcar fare. He was, all right, but the actual pattern of his experience was not so much that of the penniless boy as that of the penniless young man. He was born in Detroit, the son of a well-to-do real-estate man, and was brought up in Ann Arbor. At the age of fifteen, he entered Choate, where he had a fairly unhappy time of it. He has always found it difficult to form close friendships, and even now some of the people nearest to him regard him as uncommonly aloof. "I was very much of a mess at prep school," he says. "I was just the kind of boy parents don't want their children to be." In 1928, when he was halfway through his senior year, with his tuition only half paid up, his father, spectacularly anticipating the Depression, fell on hard times, but Choate considerately let the boy complete the year and graduate, on the house. Stevens had already applied for admission to Harvard, and was presently accepted, but his father's economic distress put an end to that plan. He enrolled instead at the University of Michigan, which, since it is in Ann Arbor, he could attend while living at home. (His mail while he was a freshman at Michigan consisted largely of invitations, forwarded from Cambridge, to débutante parties that were being given in the vicinity of Boston.) Stevens quit college after his first year, having been unable to work up an interest in his studies and having found no extracurricular activities, aside from card games, that appealed to him. He was then nineteen. "The truth of the matter is that I was quite a good-for-nothing," he says. By this time, Stevens' father was just about broke, which meant Stevens was, too. With no particular object in view, he went to Detroit, where, between 1930 and 1935—the limits of what was indisputably his hard-knocks period—he lived as best he could. He took various odd jobs; he sold a pint or so of his blood every now and then; and for one four-month stretch, he worked on a Ford assembly line. His job there was to grab one-and-a-half-inch rough-finished gears off a belt as it passed by him, and hold them against a moving steel brush to rub the burr off. While he was thus employed, the management began to accelerate the plant's output—the famous Ford speedup of that era. Stevens tried valiantly to keep pace with the belt as it flowed toward him at an

When Elia Kazan read Robert Anderson's *Tea and Sympathy* early in 1953, he quickly recommended it to Robert Sherwood of the Playwrights' Company. Anderson was asked to become a member of the Company, which presented the play less than nine months later in New York under Kazan's direction. Color poster. *Roger L. Stevens Collection, Music Division, Library of Congress.*

increasing rate, for he was getting thirty dollars a week, which was good pay then, but after two weeks of the speedup, by which time the brush had rubbed as much skin off his hands as burr off the gears, he was fired in the course of a general layoff.

For a while after this, Stevens has two jobs. By day, he worked as a real-estate broker; his commissions after six months totalled exactly nothing. By night, he worked at a gas station, where the rewards—twelve dollars a week—were more satisfying. In what off hours he had, he took to frequenting public libraries, for his attitude toward the acquisition of knowledge had changed markedly. "I read all the stuff I should have read in college but probably wouldn't have read in college," he says. At first, he was guided in his selections by a schoolteacher who had a room in the boarding house he had moved into, and before long he was reading four or five books a week of his own choice. His choice ran mostly to works by Fielding, Joyce, Mann, Wolfe, Proust, Shakespeare, Shaw, and Pirandello. He has been a relentless and retentive reader ever since. "Of all the things that can make a person happy, I'd put literature first," he says. "Many people need other people around them, but I don't if I've got books. I like the people in books better than most people I know." Stevens sometimes amazes the people he knows by saying to them—as he abruptly said to one flabbergasted mortgage broker recently—"Have you read 'Decline of the West' lately?" Once, while discussing with a friend a speech on the future of investment properties that Stevens was preparing to deliver before an audience of a hundred and fifty corporation presidents, he said, "I'm going to surprise them. I'm going to start out by quoting Marx. Well, not really Marx. I never could read him. He always put me to sleep. But I've read Strachey on Marx, and I'm going to start with a reference to that. Do you think I'm crazy? Most people start off speeches by telling jokes, but I don't know any jokes." Another friend of Stevens' said recently, "Roger has a consuming ambition to win recognition on an intellectual level. He'd rather have a good notice from Atkinson than make a mint. My guess is that he's trying to prove to himself that not going to Harvard didn't make any difference."

Toward the end of 1934, Stevens, undeterred by the failure of his first efforts to sell property, became a broker with a large Detroit real-estate firm. The real-estate market was just beginning to show signs of resurrection after the dead days of the Depression, and Stevens quickly demonstrated that he had a knack for analyzing properties, sensing which ones were undervalued and then trading profitably in those. During the last six months of 1935, he earned ten thousand dollars in commissions, and from then on he was rolling. Much of his business was in apartment-house bonds, which, as a result of the Depression, were selling at only a tiny fraction of their face value. When Stevens saw something that looked promising, he would approach a likely investor and offer to waive his commission; instead, he suggested, he would split with the investor whatever profits might result, and would agree that he was not to receive anything until the investor had realized a fifty-per-cent return on his money. Frequently, to the gratification of both Stevens and his client, the original investment increased at the rate of several hundred per cent a year. By 1937, when Stevens was twenty-six, he had been in and out of a lot of apartment houses, was making twenty-five thousand dollars a year, and had accumulated a nest egg of fifty thousand. "I wish I'd been ten years older then," he said not long ago. "Any mature person with any brains could have made a lot of money."

Closings and Openings–II

A possibly apocryphal story in the gossipy world of bankers, and other dealers in large figures concerns a meeting some time back of two real-estate men who themselves deal in figures that are not exactly small—William Zeckendorf and Roger Lacey Stevens. According to the story, Zeckendorf and Stevens, who between them control some three hundred million dollars' worth of property, were comparing notes one day, and in the course of their conversation Zeckendorf remarked, "You know, Roger, I believe you're the greatest operator of them all," whereupon Stevens, who habitually wears an air of diffidence, at once replied, "Oh, no, Bill, *you* are." Zeckendorf unexpectedly took him up on it, saying, "O.K., Roger, I guess you're right. But if I'm the greatest, you're the second greatest." Shortly after this conversation is supposed to have taken place, Stevens organized a syndicate that bought the Empire State Building for fifty-one and a half million dollars, the highest price ever paid for a single building in the history of the world, and it was not long after that that Zeckendorf's company, Webb & Knapp, Inc., bought the Chrysler Building and enough satellite buildings to bring the total price to an even fifty-two million. Stevens has been content to let Zeckendorf have the higher price tag as long as he has the higher structure. "You can juggle figures all you like," he once said, "but there is only one Empire State Building."

Whatever their ranking, Zeckendorf and Stevens are quite a pair, and comparisons between them are made with some frequency these days. Actually, they are not at all alike. Stevens, a casually dressed, soft-spoken, fairly inarticulate man of unassuming appearance, spends at least half his time not dealing in real estate at all but putting on Broadway shows; in the past, his flair for making money on closing profitable real-estate deals has been neatly balanced by a flair for losing it on opening unprofitable shows("Mr. Pickwick," "An Enemy of the People," and "Barefoot in Athens," among others), although this season, having been largely responsible for the production of such hits as "Tea and Sympathy" and "Sabrina Fair," he seems to have learned the trick of coming out on top whether he is closing a deal or opening a show. Zeckendorf, an impeccably tailored, stentorian, eloquent man with a flamboyant air, is his own show. His office, elegantly decorated with trick lighting fixtures and captive trees, and densely populated with suave staff assistants, looks like something out of *House & Garden*, his home looks like something out of "Kind Sir," and he shuttles between these two dazzling establishments in an elongated limousine (a Chrysler) with the legend "1-WZ" on its license plate. Stevens has a staff of only two people, who share with him a cramped and grubby cubicle in the Empire State Building that he has borrowed from a window washer; his files are kept not in custom-built cabinets, as Zeckendorf's are, but in old cardboard packing cartons strewn about the floor. Stevens does not have a car in New York (where, conceivably to Zeckendorf's chagrin, the words "Empire State" are inscribed on the license plate of everybody's car, including his own Chrysler), and his home here is an eight-room apartment, which, although he, his wife, their fifteen-year-old daughter, and a fourteen-year-old poodle have been living in it for a year now, is still only half furnished. Zeckendorf, a man who travels widely, confers with his real-estate associates by telephone every weekday, no matter what distant part of the world he may be in. Stevens also gets about, but he is inclined to neglect to let his associates know where he is, with the result that he is sometimes unavailable to them for a week at a stretch, even though he may be physically no more remote than Hartford.

Zeckendorf says that the only resemblance between Stevens and himself is that they are both bald. "And at that he's thin and I'm fat," he adds. This is a relative estimate. Zeckendorf's eating habits are those of a determined gourmet, verging at times on those of a gourmand. Stevens can take fancy foods or leave them alone—when he has a play in production, and his stomach is jumpy, he has been known to subsist exclusively on Martinis, pea soup, and cheese—but, notwithstanding Zeckendorf's charitable appraisal of his bulk, he too has a tendency toward stoutness. From time to time, Stevens tries to combat this by killing his appetite with tobacco, to which he has a long-standing antipathy. When he is in a reducing mood, he smokes quantities of cigars. "I loathe the damn things," he once said while lifting up an innocuous-looking stogie. There is no one brand that he particularly detests; he will puff, and gag, on any old kind, provided that it does not strike him as ineffectually bland.

Stevens and Zeckendorf run into each other every now and then. At one meeting a couple of years ago, Zeckendorf, who, at forty-eight, refers to Stevens, who is forty-three, as a "young man," suggested that they pool their formidable talents. Stevens was to take over Zeckendorf's job as president of Webb and Knapp, and Zeckendorf would

Robert Whitehead has long been one of the theatre's most loved and respected producers. He came to be associated with Roger Stevens early in Stevens's theatre career, and remained in partnership with him until Stevens's death in 1998. *Theatre Arts*, April 1955. *General Collections, Library of Congress.*

become chairman of its board. Had the proposed merger gone through, it would probably have had an effect on real estate similar to the one that the creation of United States Steel had on heavy industry, but Stevens declined the offer, feeling that both he and Zeckendorf operate best in the role of lone, if far from hungry, wolves. As competitors, moreover, they have a livelier relationship than they might have as partners. Last fall, soon after Zeckendorf picked up the Chrysler Building, Stevens and some of his co-proprietors of the Empire State Building invited him to lunch in their building in order to congratulate him in a straightforward, if unavoidably condescending, way on owning the second-highest building in the world. They even arranged a press conference to commemorate the occasion. This was held in a room where scale models of the two buildings rested on a table behind which the guest of honor, and various of his hosts, could be photographed. With no half mile in between to soften the contrast, as there is in real, life, the Chrysler Building looked pathetically puny alongside the Empire State. Zeckendorf stalked fearlessly into this enemy territory, stole the ensuing headlines by answering all the questions that were asked by the reporters (he later said that he had waited politely for his hosts to answer them, but that they had seemed to be struck dumb in his presence), and, when the photographers aimed their cameras, came within a hair of achieving a really remarkable triumph by deftly picking up the model of the Chrysler Building, as if to examine it, and elevating its spire above that of the model of the Empire State. "The damn-fool photographers muffed it," he lamented afterward.

Although Stevens attended the party for Zeckendorf, he rarely turns up for the receptions that are held at the Empire State Building for other distinguished visitors, like the touring royalty, who come to see it and the view from it. "I try to duck that sort of thing," he explained recently. "It's too time-consuming. I haven't been on top of the tower in a year." His first ascent was made a couple of years ago, when he and some of his colleagues were being shown around shortly before they were to take over the premises. Construction on the television mast was then in progress, and the new owners were led to some scaffolding, which consisted of narrow planks of wood edged with chicken wire, and were urged to walk around the tower on it. Stevens, who suffers mildly from acrophobia, looked down, turned green, clutched a nearby metal upright, and said, "You boys walk around. I'll wait." Later, he picked out as his office a cubbyhole, no more than eight feet wide and twenty long, on the fifth floor.

Stevens never puts himself out to dispel the impression that the course of his career has been the classical rags-to-riches one, although as the son of a once prosperous Detroit real-estate man who was all but wiped out during the late twenties, he has a followed a course that might be more accurately described as riches-to-rags-to-riches. It was riches to rags when, because his father was unable to send him on to Harvard after he graduated from Choate, he kicked around Detroit during the early thirties, living in furnished rooms, reading in public libraries, and barely supporting himself by a miscellany of odd jobs. Once he got into the straight rags-to-riches stretch of the course, however, he followed the conventional pattern by getting married as soon as he felt he had enough money in the bank. That was in 1938. Stevens, who had been flat broke three years earlier, and had spent the intervening time amassing fifty thousand dollars by some brilliant broken-field running in the Detroit real-estate market, met Christine Gesell, a native of St. Louis, at a party in Ann Arbor, where the Stevens family had been living for some years. Her family had moved to that town when she was five, and she had just finished her sophomore year at the University of Michigan. She told Stevens that she wanted to leave school and get a secretarial job, and Stevens, somewhat mellowed by the party, said grandly, "I'll find you one." Despite a flowery recommendation he wrote for her, she was turned down everywhere she went, for her qualifications were not imposing; she didn't know shorthand and could barely type. Finally, Stevens gallantly hired her himself. Then he went off on a business trip. When he got back, he discovered that she had furnished his office with a hideous, eggplant-colored carpet. Soon thereafter, they got married, and since by then neither of them could stand the sight of the carpet, they took half his savings and set out on a six-month honeymoon trip around the world. When they got back, they settled in Ann Arbor, and Stevens, with the cooperation of a constantly widening circle of affluent acquaintances, resumed his real-estate activities in Detroit. Among the investors with whom he had frequent dealings were Ben Tobin and Alfred R. Glancy, Jr., two Detroiters who have been closely linked with his destiny ever since. In the world of real estate, the three men are often spoken of collectively as the Detroit Syndicate. Tobin is an authentic rags-to-riches man. He came to this country from Russia as a boy of ten, got his start in the business world by selling newspapers in Lynn, Massachusetts, and is now the owner of the Hollenden Hotel in Cleveland and the Hollywood Beach Hotel in Florida. Glancy is a riches-to-more-riches man. His father, now retired, was for many years the head of the Pontiac Division of General Motors. The son graduated from Princeton in 1932 and tried to get a job in a Detroit bank–any Detroit bank. For all his father's connections, the banks weren't hiring anybody, but young Glancy persuaded one of them to take him on without pay. To give himself the feeling of being remuneratively employed, he deposited a large sum in the bank, and every payday the bank gave him a check against his own account. Then the bank failed, costing Glancy not only his job but his payroll money. Not long afterward, he began handling some of his family's investments, and was soon putting a good deal of glancy money into attractive real-estate propositions that Stevens called to his attention.

Tobin conducted a real-estate business from an office in the Tuller Hotel in Detroit. One day in 1941, Stevens, who was trying to arrange for a client to lease that hotel, was riding in one of its elevators with some of the other participants in the deal when he suddenly became fed up with the slowness of the negotiations. He hopped out of the elevator at the next floor. Strolling down a corridor, he passed Tobin's office, and, having met him casually, stopped in to say hello. "Once I was there, I had to have something to talk about," Stevens said recently. "Well, I happened to remember that the Hollenden Hotel in Cleveland was up for sale, cheap, so I said, 'You know, I think I can buy the Hollenden for you and arrange to have it leased, so you won't have to operate it, and get you thirty per cent on your investment.' The next thing you know, Ben owned the Hollenden. We had some trouble with the people who were supposed to take the lease from him, so I told Al Glancy about it, and he and I ended up as Ben's lessees. After a year and a half, Ben refinanced the hotel, and he was able to borrow enough money on it to buy the Hollywood Beach for a million and a half. The Hollywood Beach is now worth five or six million. And all this came about because I got bored in an elevator. The Tuller thing worked out fine, too, after that lucky slow start. I was trying to broker the deal, and I had a four o'clock deadline for a twenty-five-thousand-dollar deposit my client had promised to put up. At three-forty-five, I was still shy a third of that, and the guy representing the owner said to me, 'If you're so anxious to close this deal and think it's so good, why don't you put up the rest yourself?' I said sure. I put up the third, and later sold half of my interest to another broker. I gave the other half to my wife, and the property went up so much in value that she's been making twenty-five thousand a year on it ever since. That's known as the deal of deals in Detroit."

At about the time the deal of deals went through, the United States went to war. Stevens wanted a commission in the Navy, but he found that his lack of a college degree was a big obstacle. He consulted a Navy acquaintance, who advised him forthrightly, "Tell them how much money you make, and I'm sure they'll be interested." Stevens told them, and was duly commissioned. He spent two years at a Naval air station near Miami Beach, supervising a crew that kept oxygen equipment shipshape. While there, he picked up a lot of information about resort hotels, and upon returning to civilian life and the real-estate business he, with Glancy and some other colleagues, bought four of them—three in Florida and one at Myrtle Beach, South Carolina. Stevens has never spent much time in any of his hotels; he is not the sort of man to enjoy lounging around lobbies and bowing to transients. His sole interest in hotels is financial.

In 1949, when Stevens invaded New York, Glancy and Tobin marched sturdily at his side. The trio formed a corporation here and, for eight million dollars, most of it borrowed, took over Realty Associates, Inc., a fifty-year-old real-estate firm whose affairs were being liquidated; with the firm, they acquired an assortment of assets, including the Brooklyn Paramount Theatre and nearly half of the Hotel Taft. They made handsome profits. The three partners no longer have any formal corporate identity, but they have continued to collaborate from time to time, and recently they were prominent in a group that bought the Squibb Building for ten million dollars, a sum that hardly made any of them think twice.

In the days when Stevens was primarily a hotel owner, he never found it easy to get a room at the Ritz-Carlton in Boston. He considers it significant that now, as a theatrical producer who frequently takes shows to Boston, he not only can get into the Ritz himself but can get friends in. As he sees it, his altered standing with the management there is symptomatic of the advantages a man of culture and commerce enjoys over a man of unrelieved commerce. Disinterested observers, however, have pointed out that Stevens has lately had plans afoot to put up a seventy-five-million-dollar business center in Boston, and that this may have something to do with the cordiality of his reception at the Ritz. The idea of the center, which is by far the most ambitious undertaking he has tackled yet, came to him about a year ago. No matter where he is, he views the landscape with a real-estate man's eye, and during his frequent trips to Boston in the interests of the theatre he fell to brooding about the vast and dreary yards of the Boston & Albany Railroad, which cover twenty-eight acres of

One of the first productions on which Stevens and Whitehead worked together was *The Remarkable Mr. Pennypacker*, which opened at the Morosco Theatre in New York on December 30, 1953, with Burgess Meredith (shown here) in the lead, and in London on May 18, 1955, at the New Theatre with Nigel Patrick as Pa Pennypacker. *Theatre Arts*, April 1955. General Collections, Library of Congress.

the Back Bay section, or more than twice the area of Radio City. Last spring after a number of conferences with the mayor of Boston and other influential citizens, Stevens announced that he had taken an option on the land and proposed to use it as a site for four office buildings, ranging in height from seven to forty stories; an eighteen-story hotel, with a motel attached; garages to accommodate six thousand cars; a supermarket to accommodate seventy thousand shoppers; and random swimming pools, ice-skating rinks, dance pavilions, and exhibit halls. He has organized a cartel of architects, among them Walter Gropius, to plan this enterprising project, which he hopes will attract housewives from all the myriad suburbs of Boston. He is aware that this hope runs counter to the current trend of decentralization in shopping, but he takes a confident stand in defense of his position. "I think women like the romance of going downtown to shop," he says.

Stevens is uncommonly indifferent to money. "I never try to accumulate it, I just like to fling it about," he remarked once. In flinging it about, though, he has never in return picked up very many of the costly possessions that some men of means tend to collect. He lives simply. The only home he owns is a six-room house in Ann Arbor where he goes weekends whenever he can and where he keeps his only car, a Plymouth. The house, which he bought shortly after his marriage, is worth about fifteen thousand dollars. He was momentarily unhappy when *Time* reported that he had received a hundred and sixty-six thousand dollars as a broker's commission on his syndicate's purchase of the Empire State: he explained to a friend that he feared the report would give his neighbors in Ann Arbor the wrong impression of him. (He did not say what he thought their impression would have been if *Time* had printed the correct figure—two hundred and fifty thousand.) Stevens just does not care how much money he has, and often he does not know. He was mildly surprised, but not upset, when his accountant, after balancing his income and outgo for 1952, which Stevens had thought was one of his better years, told him that he had forty thousand dollars less at its end than at its beginning.

The decline of Stevens' personal fortune that year was partly the result of his becoming deeply involved in politics. As chairman of the finance committee of the National Volunteers for Stevenson, he was one of the Democrats' principal fund raisers. (He has been a Democrat all his adult life, having been profoundly moved during his library-reading days by the works of Lincoln Steffens and of such New Deal philosophers as Thurman Arnold and Jerome Frank.) Although most of his business associates were Republicans, he kept badgering them for Stevenson money. He didn't get much from them, but he and his fellow-volunteers did collect almost a million dollars elsewhere. Quite a bit of this was contributed in small sums, and all of it was funneled into an office that was then shared by Stevens, Glancy, and Tobin. Glancy, a resolute Republican, could get to his desk only by wading through twenty or thirty young lady volunteers who were ripping open envelopes and shaking out Democratic dollar bills.

The Democratic Party was not the only special cause that dented Stevens' personal resources in 1952. He also made some rather large contributions to what he calls "Christine's animal stuff." This is a reference to the Animal Welfare Institute, a non-profit corporation of which Mrs. Stevens is the founder and president and her husband the treasurer, and which has its national headquarters in the Empire State Building. (The long-suffering Glancy is vice-president of the Institute, even though his attitude toward the well-being of animals is passive, to say the least.) Within the confines of the animal-welfare world, which is itself rather restricted, Mrs. Stevens, who is the daughter of Dr. Robert Gesell, a physiologist at the University of Michigan, and the niece of Dr. Arnold Gesell, the famous child psychologist at Yale, is widely recognized as a controversial crusader. Her appearance belies her reputation. She is a gentle, delicate-featured, soft-voiced woman of thirty-five who has always had a friendly feeling toward the smaller mammals. She founded the Animal Welfare Institute, which is pretty much a one-woman outfit, three years ago, in the belief that there was a pressing need for an organization that could occupy the no man's land lying between the embattled forces of the vivisectionists, who are vehemently opposed to any experiments whatever on live animals, and the medical-research people, who feel they have a right to all the animals they think they need and aren't universally worried about the sensitivities of those they get. Mrs. Stevens does not object to the use of animals in experimental laboratories, holding that this is necessary for the advancement of science, but she contends that these animals should be treated humanely and that the ones that must die should die painlessly. "The middle course must prevail!" is the motto of her Institute.

The middle course is a hard one to steer, as Ulysses learned long ago. Mrs. Stevens' Scylla is the New York State Society for Medical Research, which passed a formal resolution a year ago calling upon its members to have no truck with her Institute; her Charybdis is the International Conference Against Vivisection, which recently distributed a circular denouncing her and her organization. Many doctors think she is little better than an antivivisectionist herself; the antivivisectionists assert that she is the daughter of a vivisectionist, and hint darkly that she maintains a secret experimental laboratory of her own. She does not, but she concedes that her father's professional research

Thomas Stearns Eliot's *The Confidential Clerk*, with Ina Claire and Claude Rains was presented by the Producers' Theatre in New York on February 11, 1954. Stevens was associated with American premieres of a number of pieces of poetic theatre, including works by Eliot and Christopher Fry. *Theatre Arts*, April 1955. *General Collections, Library of Congress.*

requires him to use animals. "I am the daughter of a *kindly* vivisectionist," she says.

Stevens plays a modest role in the activities of the Institute. Besides providing it with rent-free office space and supplying a substantial part of the funds needed to make up its deficits, he faithfully attends its annual directors' meetings. Since he is a busy man, the most recent one lasted only thirty seconds. (Stevens has been known to appear at the meeting of a corporation's board of directors just long enough to stick his head inside the door and shout "I vote 'yes,'" before scurrying on to another engagement.) Now and then, he accompanies his wife to conventions of humane associations, where the atmosphere around her often crackles with acrimony. "The intrigues at the United Nations are nothing compared to what goes on at some of those meetings," Stevens said recently. "Why, the doctors and druggists are boring from within now! They've infiltrated the A.S.P.C.A.!"

In theory, Stevens devotes his mornings to real estate and his afternoons and evenings to the theatre, but in practice the two become hopelessly interwoven. As a non-playwriting member of the Playwrights' Company, he may find himself called upon any morning to give an opinion on a script before noon, and as president and treasurer of the new million-dollar Producers' Theatre, with its ambitious plans to produce plays the year round in the three New York theatres it controls, he finds himself involved in both real estate and the drama on a round-the-clock basis. (Not long ago, Stevens kept himself incommunicado all one morning, afternoon, and evening—while bankers and brokers and playwrights and actors tried frantically to track him down—because he was having temperament trouble with the cast of "Ondine," the opening of which was drawing uncomfortably near.) Stevens' chaotic jumbling of his two careers, while perhaps to a degree inevitable, is intensified by the fact that he administers his affairs with a glorious disregard for system. His tiny staff, which is probably the tiniest any skyscraper owner ever had, consists of one male adjutant and one female secretary. The adjutant, Nathan S. Potter III, a real-estate expert in his own right, grew up with Stevens in Ann Arbor, and, before he switched to his present position, worked for General Motors, another big operator. The secretary, Patricia Foley, joined Stevens six years ago, in Detroit, where he was then spending most of his time. While she is no great shakes as a typist and only a middling curator of files, as both she and her employer amiably admit, she is adept at placating out-of-town real-estate men who want opening night tickets at the last minute. Stevens' abhorrence of administrative detail drives some of his friends almost to distraction. Although he has occupied his office in the Empire State Building for two years now, he has not yet bothered to order any stationery with that address, and most of his business letters are written on some old Detroit letterheads he brought along when he came East, with "Empire State Building" typed on by Miss Foley at the top. And last year, shortly after Stevens organized a firm called the Stevens Development Corporation,

Audrey Hepburn and Mel Ferrer in *Ondine* by Jean Giraudoux. The play was a tragic fantasy about the love of a water sprite for a human, a medieval knight. It opened on February 17, 1954, at New York's 46th Street Theatre. World Telegram and Sun *Collection, Prints and Photographs Division, Library of Congress.*

with himself as president, to promote the contemplated center in Boston, one of his associates in the venture was dismayed to find that he was trying to raise the millions of dollars needed for it with letters written on paper that had no letterhead at all and wasn't even bond. The associate had a batch of crisp, substantial-looking stationery printed up and persuaded Stevens to accept a couple of hundred sheets, which he is now grudgingly using.

This distaste for fancy letter paper may derive from Stevens' dislike of business documents in general. Eighty per cent of his deals, he says, are clinched by oral agreements, the legal rituals that follow being little more than formalities, even if often tedious and protracted ones. "In spite of Arthur Miller and all the rest of them, the basis of big business is trust," he says. In the course of the negotiations that preceded his taking over the Empire State Building, he got into a debate with Frederick H. Ecker, the honorary chairman of the board of the Metropolitan Life Insurance Company, who was then eighty-four years old and is still going strong. The Metropolitan held a mortgage on the Empire State, and Stevens was anxious to prepay some interest due on it, to clear the decks for transferring the ownership of the building. There was some disagreement over the amount involved, and Ecker, a very shrewd and vigorous gentleman who acts as if his chairmanship were anything but honorary, announced during a discussion of this matter that he was going to be governed by an oral agreement he had made many years earlier with the late John J. Raskob, who built the Empire State, and not by any clauses, however impressive, that Stevens' lawyers might dredge out of any old documents. Stevens forthwith dropped the argument, even though this meant a loss of close to four hundred thousand dollars to him and his associates. His concession to Ecker was based partly on his eagerness to get over that particular hurdle, some of his friends maintain, but also on his having been charmed into acquiescence by the old man's veneration for the spoken pledge.

Stevens thinks so little of written documents that he has to be constantly cautioned against signing them without reading them. His attitude toward appointment schedules is equally cavalier. He makes appointments readily, but then things crowd in on him and he gets running behind time. His real-estate business these days often calls for simultaneous conferences with representatives of the banking houses of J. P. Morgan & Co. and Hemphill, Noyes & Co. and the legal firm of Cravath, Swaine & Moore, all three of them situated within a couple of downtown blocks. Stevens is so apt to be tardy that nobody ever shows up for one of these conferences, which are usually held in the board room of one or another of the three firms, until he arrives; then word is flashed to the interested parties, and they converge upon him. In the meantime, the switchboards at all three august institutions are likely to have been uncommonly abuzz for hours with importuning calls for Stevens from actors' agents, salesmen of asbestos curtains, and mothers of ingénues, for he is almost constantly on the go, and like a busy doctor, can only be reached by messages placed along his probable course. In consequence, as he finally sits down in the Morgan board room, glancing as he does so at one of the messages awaiting him there, he may begin the conference by exclaiming, "Oh, God! Now the leading lady won't talk to the leading man!"

In his real-estate maneuverings, Stevens is singularly unruffled by anxieties that might ruffle other men badly. "Roger just never lets anything bother him," an investment banker on his downtown circuit said recently. "Most other people couldn't take the risks he does without worrying all the time. In a sense, there's nothing for him to worry about, because he goes into big deals for the fun of it. Business is a game to him—he's dead set on winning, mind you, but it's still a game. He makes it fun for you, too, because in dealing with him you never have to concern yourself about what you'll get out of it. If there's anything in a deal at all, you know he's going to treat you well. As a matter of fact, you sometimes wonder if he's keeping track of how he'll come out himself." Stevens never had more of his rather special kind of fun than when he was buying the Empire State Building. The principal but by no means only players on his team in this particular game were Glancy and Tobin. The big building had been erected in 1931, at a cost of fifty-two million of that era's dollars. It didn't do well financially for a decade, but by the early forties it had begun to show a profit. Its annual net income is now more than five million dollars. In 1950, when Raskob died, roughly eighty per cent of the Empire State's stock was owned by his estate and his relatives; ten per cent by the relatives of Alfred E. Smith, the buildings first president; and the remainder by scattered shareholders. In 1951, the owners of the majority of the behemoth's stock decided to put it up for sale.

Stevens, who sometimes says he was attracted to the Empire State Building solely because it seemed to be a cheap piece of real estate, got wind of the fact that it might be available when he stopped in at Hemphill, Noyes one morning in the spring of 1951 to pass the time of day with Jansen Noyes, Jr., one of the three Noyes members of the firm. "Why don't we stir something up?" Stevens asked conversationally. Noyes had just been told, in hushed, furtive tones, by a vice-president of the Charles F. Noyes Company, a real-estate brokerage firm, that the Empire State Building might be on the market, and he now relayed this news, in a whisper, to Stevens. (While Charles Noyes is not related to the Hemphill, Noyes Noyeses, they have many dealings with his company and invariably refer to him as Uncle Charlie.) Stevens said in an offhand manner that he would be interested in seeing the building's audited statement and hearing a price, but Jansen Noyes hadn't been let in on any such arcane figures. A month later, Uncle Charlie visited Hemphill, Noyes and disclosed that the prospective sellers wanted fifty million dollars, take it or leave it. (This proved to be the final selling price; the extra million and a half went for lawyers' fees and other costs incidental to the change of ownership.) Jansen Noyes asked if he could convey this information, together with a few other statistics that Uncle Charlie had guardedly passed along, to a certain individual, and when Uncle Charlie consented, he telephoned Stevens, who was then in Detroit. In a strangely unfamiliar voice, Stevens instructed Noyes to take an option on the building for himself, Glancy, and Tobin. Noyes expected Stevens to come directly to New York to go into details, but he had no further word from him for three weeks. Noyes later learned that at the time of his telephone call Stevens had had the mumps, and had been too embarrassed about his predicament to mention it or to show himself on Wall Street.

Stevens made a million-dollar deposit on the Empire State Building in May, 1951, and agreed to hand over the rest of the money by November 30th. In accepting the down payment, the attorneys for the Raskob estate, who were superintending the other end of the deal, granted him one out: He could withdraw from the whole business if the financial situation of the country changed materially before August 31st. Like many another current purchaser of large real-estate holdings, Stevens decided to raise part of the necessary cash, and reap certain attractive tax benefits, by selling the land out from under the building and then leasing the land back. He got the Metropolitan Life Insurance Company to agree to be the other party, provided he could arrange suitable mortgage financing. By mid-August, J. P. Morgan & Co. had promised Stevens a two-and-a-half-million-dollar loan, and he had a few more million dollars half promised, but he was still far short of his objective. His attempts to obtain mortgage money had got nowhere. Stevens nevertheless announced to all concerned that in his opinion financial conditions had not changed and that he considered himself committed to go ahead. It has since been widely conceded that he was taking a monumental risk. Mortgage money in the amount that he required—somewhere around twenty million dollars was the sum he had settled on as enough—was extremely tight. But Stevens, whose sensitivity to the nuances of the money market is considered acute, knew that toward autumn some of the big insurance companies are usually loaded down with incoming premium money that they haven't yet got around to investing and are in search of ways to unload it. Before tackling any such source of help, he persuaded the Raskob estate to take a five-million-dollar purchase-money second mortgage. Then, although he had been turned down twice by the Prudential Insurance Company—or, as it is usually called in financial circles, the Pru—on a twenty-million-dollar first leasehold mortgage, he approached it again, for he had reason to believe that it was eager to find outlets for uninvested funds. This time, he asked the Prudential for a fifteen-and-a-half-million-dollar first mortgage and offered to pay five per cent interest—one-half per cent more than the maximum he had previously discussed. After some deliberation, the Prudential found this proposition interesting enough to give him an oral commitment on it, but only if he would also switch to it the land-sale-and-lease-back deal he had arranged with the Metropolitan. The Metropolitan graciously consented to withdraw, and the Prudential was in, tentatively, for thirty-two and a half million—the first mortgage

Audrey Hepburn in *Ondine*. The Playwrights' Theatre production was very successful as long as Hepburn stayed with it. When she left after just a few months, the show closed. *Life,* May 24, 1954. *General Collections, Library of Congress.*

and an additional seventeen million dollars for the land, or just about nine million dollars an acre. Stevens was to lease this back for a hundred years, at an annual rental that was to be a million and twenty thousand dollars for the first thirty years and to decrease over the next seventy until it amounted to a mere three hundred and forty thousand.

Although the Prudential had agreed in principle to all this, it was far from ready to hand over the money. It insisted on waiting until the lease on the land had been drawn up and carefully examined. The examination, with corollary dickering, took four solid weeks of sixteen-hour-a-day sessions, during which Stevens and his colleagues, including his lawyer, Thomas A. Halleran, a member of Cravath, Swaine & Moore, fenced with a committee of insurance executives over details. As the wrangling progressed, Stevens assumed a characteristic air of lamblike naïveté. The more the Prudential's lawyers raised their voices, the softer and more trembling his voice became. He declared abjectly that while he sympathized with the Pru's position, his lawyer, Halleran, was a temperamental dragon who, if the Pru didn't yield on its demands, might very well order him to wash his hands of the deal—a course that, by this stage of the game, Stevens felt sure the Pru had no wish to have him follow. (Stevens once asked Halleran why it was that he always seemed to get himself involved in troublesome legalities in the course of closing deals. "There's always trouble when you try to substitute ingenuity for cash," the lawyer replied.) At the end of the four weeks, Stevens got his mortgage, and the rental terms he wanted, but the Prudential's lawyers, perhaps piqued at not having won any modification of the lease—an eighty-five-page printed document that Halleran had submitted for the ratification—declined to approve it until the whole thing had been reprinted, unchanged except that the margins were a quarter of an inch wider. Reflecting on those exciting days, Tobin says, "I was scared to death. It looked as if Roger couldn't get through, but he did. If he hadn't licked the Pru, we'd have been dead. The million dollars we'd have forfeited would have been bad enough, but we could probably have offset that somehow. It was the loss of face that would have been fatal."

Meanwhile, Stevens had had to raise his equity money—fourteen million dollars, including his million-dollar deposit and the loan from J. P. Morgan. He had got Charles Noyes to come in for a million four hundred thousand by dangling before him a hundred-thousand-dollar-a-year contract to manage the Empire State Building. The Allegheny Corporation, an investment company controlled by Robert R. Young, proved good for two million one hundred thousand more. Then the Raskob and Smith families added a million fifty thousand, mostly out of sentiment. And the Stevens, Glancy, and Tobin group had something over two million dollars more of its own to throw into the kitty. Some other friends of Stevens' furnished the relatively trifling sum of three hundred and fifty thousand. There was one more large investor whom Stevens had been counting on to provide the remaining two million eight hundred thousand, but at nearly the last minute the man decided he wasn't interested. On November 28th, forty-eight hours before his deadline, Stevens advised the Raskob-estate lawyers that he guessed he'd have to forfeit, after all. Not wanting to start renegotiating all over again with a new customer, they agreed to assume this share if he would promise to try to get somebody else to take it as soon as possible. They even suggested a prospect—Colonel Henry Crown, a Chicago investor who was a director of Columbia Pictures, the Rock Island Railroad, and the Hilton Hotels. Stevens scurried right over to see Crown's New York attorney, and presently the Colonel had joined the syndicate. As a reward for his coöperativeness, he was made chairman of the board of the Empire State Building. Stevens was pleased with the way things had worked out. "By the time I was through putting the pieces together," he said later, "I had made everybody in the deal a buccaneer—each one thought he was getting the edge on everybody else." Colonel Crown must have been pleased, too, for he has since bought up the shares of a number of his associates—including most of Tobin's interest in the venture—and now owns more than half the Empire State Building, or roughly fifty-two stories.

Caricature of Alfred Lunt by Covarrubias. Lunt was considered one of the finest actors of his time. Both Lunt and his wife, Lynn Fontanne, were famous for their devotion to their art; they worked constantly on perfecting their roles, making modifications even up to closing night. *Prints and Photographs Division, Library of Congress.*

As Stevens was assembling his pieces, Halleran was feverishly preparing for the closing, which, after being postponed once to get the margins on the lease satisfactorily adjusted, was finally scheduled to get under way at nine-thirty on the morning of December 21st in the board room of the Bankers Trust Company's main offices, at 16 Wall Street. Stevens obviously couldn't sell the land out from under the building, but he couldn't buy the building until he got the proceeds from the sale of the land. Halleran concluded that these two steps, as well as a hundred and two other necessary formalities, would have to be imaged as occurring simultaneously, and he persuaded four title-insurance companies to accept this premise. Then he got up a thirty-three-page memorandum of stage directions for all the people—sellers and their lawyers, buyers and their lawyers, title-insurance-company representatives and their lawyers, notary publics and their lawyers, and others and their lawyers—who had to convene to execute the transfer of the property. This was just as well, since the transfer called for the passing back and forth of six hundred documents, bearing two thousand signatures, and the payment by one party to another of checks totalling $167,222,056.13. The strain of getting set for all this was so severe that one scheduled participant collapsed from nervous exhaustion shortly before the big day. A dress rehearsal of the closing, with the whole cast present, was held on December 20th, to make sure no one would blow his lines. "This wasn't done as a theatrical gesture," Stevens has since said. "If anything had gone wrong, all hell might have broken loose. We had to be certain the next paper in the series wouldn't be blocked because of some unforeseen legal technicality. By the day of the actual closing, I was numb. I had visions of being known for the rest of my life as the man who didn't buy the Empire State Building. It all went off without a hitch, though. There must have been a hundred people in the room when we closed, and as the last signature was put on the last piece of paper, seven and a half hours after we'd started, they all suddenly and spontaneously burst into applause. I never in my life heard anything like it except on an opening night."

Roger L. Stevens on Broadway and in the West End

Walter Zvonchenko

From the time of his earliest involvement in professional theatre, Roger L. Stevens was passionate about raising the standards of theatrical production, constantly seeking out projects and associates that could bring plays of unusually high quality to the stage. While he had a sense of the commercially viable, his primary interest clearly was in the great classics of the stage (his first presentation in New York was a production of Shakespeare's Twelfth Night at the revered old Empire Theatre, opening in October 1949) and in writers considered to be among the finest of the time. These included Thomas Stearns Eliot, Christopher Fry, Friedrich Duerrenmatt, Harold Pinter, Tennessee Williams, and Jean Giraudoux, one of the most eminent writers for the French stage in the early twentieth century and the playwright for whom he reserved his greatest interest and enthusiasm. He began producing on Broadway when he was already a prominent figure in real estate. He very quickly established himself as a major power in the theatre, active both in the United States and Britain. He had a remarkable ability to grasp quickly the most important elements and players in any situation he chose to undertake, building around these a sound administrative and financial structure which very often brought ultimate success to his efforts. He had an overwhelming enthusiasm for the theatre, bringing to it an enormous intensity, intelligence, and thoroughness.

Stevens produced in the theatre both independently and through a number of companies and was also active in theatre ownership and management. In addition to presenting new American works on Broadway, he was active in presenting American plays in Britain, and bringing British and Continental works to the United States. All of this while simultaneously continuing his vast real estate operations, which involved a number of very large-scale projects.

Stevens's dramatic rise to the top echelon among producers in a very short space of time is all the more remarkable since, apart from his association in the 1940s with a theatre group in Ann Arbor, Michigan, he had no theatre experience until he brought a production of *Twelfth Night,* with a professional acting company, from Ann Arbor to New York to positive critical reception.

After coproducing a revival of James Barrie's *Peter Pan*, with music by Leonard Bernstein, starring Jean Arthur as Peter, at the Imperial Theatre in New York beginning April 24, 1950, he became associated

The Golden Apple, which had its premiere at New York's Phoenix Theatre on March 11, 1954, won the Donaldson and New York Drama Critics Circle Awards for best musical of the 1953-1954 season. It had been written some time earlier with the support of a Guggenheim Fellowship, but initially a producer could not be found. *Lucy Kroll Collection, Manuscript Division, Library of Congress.*

The Golden Apple was presented entirely in song and mime. Taking elements from Homer's *Odyssey* and *Iliad*, it was set in the State of Washington after the Spanish-American War, with characters whose names reflected ancient Greek mythology. *Lucy Kroll Collection, Manuscript Division, Library of Congress.*

with the American National Theatre and Academy. He worked there with the well-respected producer and director Robert Whitehead, who became head of ANTA in 1952. Stevens and Whitehead formed a relationship which lasted until Stevens's death in 1998. In 1951, John Wharton, a founding member of the Playwrights' Company, initiated discussion with Stevens about including Stevens as a member of the company, a group founded in 1938 by Robert Sherwood, Maxwell Anderson, S. N. Behrman, Elmer Rice, and Wharton to foster productions of plays written by the members, who were some of the best-known playwrights of the time. Then in 1953, Stevens joined with Robert Whitehead and Robert Dowling to form the Producers' Theatre. Dowling, like Stevens, was a well-known real estate figure with an interest in theatre. He headed City Investing, which owned a number of theatres in New York, including, at one point, the Morosco, Coronet, and Fulton, managed by a subsidiary group, City Playhouses. Stevens became involved with City Investing. City Playhouses theatres

The Golden Apple. Paris, a traveling salesman, arrives in Angels' Roost in the State of Washington. Paris fascinates Helen, wife of the town sheriff. She runs off to Rhododendron with him. Helen was played by Kaye Ballard, who was the biggest star to come out of the production. *Lucy Kroll Collection, Manuscript Division, Library of Congress.*

The Golden Apple. Rhododendron's ladies of pleasure in "By Goona-Goona Lagoon," one of the production's best-remembered moments, with Bibi Osterwald as Lovey Mars. Hanya Holm's choreography was considered a standout, as were the colorful sets by William and Jean Eckhart. *Lucy Kroll Collection, Manuscript Division, Library of Congress*

The Golden Apple. Composer Jerome Moross, lyricist John Latouche, Jonathan Lucas as Paris, and Kaye Ballard as Helen. Homer, on whose work the production is rather loosely based, is at center. *Life*, May 24, 1954. *General Collections, Library of Congress.*

were home to a considerable number of stage productions in which Stevens had an interest.

It was also in these early years as a producer that Stevens began long-term associations with some of the foremost producers, theatre managers, and artists in midcentury in London's West End, the heart of British theatre. The Roger Stevens papers in the Library of Congress include documentation on Stevens's London/Broadway connections, and testify to Stevens's constant pursuit of excellence in the theatre. Stevens's extraordinary grasp of a wide range of aspects of theatre operation is reflected in these materials, perhaps most particularly in his exchanges with Hugh Beaumont, the leading producing figure of British theatre of the time. The letters to and from Beaumont offer a splendid insight into the interaction between Stevens and Beaumont about plans to bring American plays to London and British productions to New York, especially during the 1950s when Stevens's theatrical activities were at a particularly fervent pitch. Those were the years when his time was not yet so taken up with affairs in Washington. At the height of their careers, Stevens and Beaumont both had a large number of projects under way or under consideration at any given time, and their correspondence provides a great amount of sharing of news and rumors, and fears and expectations about plays, personalities, and theatre booking.

The correspondence in Stevens's papers affords a splendid and fascinating overview of theatre history of the time—discussions of several productions, of bookings, of stars of the greatest magnitude and equally well-known and respected directors and designers.

The correspondence is also a chronicle of frequent disparity of taste between London and New York theatregoers. Often, a success in one city was a failure in the other.

This essay touches briefly on a small number of stage productions or projects with which Stevens was involved in his London-New York associations. But the persistent theme is Stevens's high standards and his hopes for theatre of the utmost quality.

Among Stevens's associates in London were the producer Henry Sherek, with whom Stevens presented T. S. Eliot's *The Confidential*

Horton Foote's *The Traveling Lady* was one of several plays associated with Stevens in which the renowned Kim Stanley starred. Others included *Picnic, Chéri, Bus Stop, A Clearing in the Woods*, the London *Cat on a Hot Tin Roof, A Far Country*, and *A Touch of the Poet*. Lucy Kroll Collection, Manuscript Division, Library of Congress.

Burl Ives, as Big Daddy, watches a birthday tribute engineered by his daughter-in-law Mae in *Cat on a Hot Tin Roof*, one of Tennessee Williams's and the Playwrights' Company's most successful plays. It opened in New York at the Morosco Theatre on March 24, 1955. *Theatre Arts*, July 1955. *General Collections, Library of Congress.*

Clerk in New York City, Laurence Olivier, and Prince Littler. Littler administered a number of the leading theatres in London, including the Globe, which housed headquarters for the producing firm of H. M. Tennent Ltd., the leading producing company in London at the mid-decades of the twentieth century. Founded in 1936, Tennent was headed by Beaumont when Stevens became involved in the West End. Beaumont was the single greatest force in theatrical production in Britain at the time, and was famous and respected for the high quality of production values which be demanded and brought to the plays he presented. In this drive for quality, he was a splendid complement to Stevens. Stevens also worked with the American producer Gilbert Miller, who had a long-standing producing career in London, owned London's St. James Theatre, and had an interest in ownership of the Lyric, one of the theatres frequently housing Tennent productions.

Tennessee Williams and Elia Kazan in Philadelphia during the pre-Broadway run of *Cat on a Hot Tin Roof*. Barbara Bel Geddes and Burl Ives are seated behind them. Stevens was associated with Williams in other presentations, including *The Milk Train Doesn't Stop Here Anymore*. *Theatre Arts,* July 1955. *General Collections, Library of Congress.*

Barbara Bel Geddes, Mildred Dunnock, Madeleine Sherwood, Pat Hingle, and Ben Gazzara in the New York production of *Cat on a Hot Tin Roof*. Stevens pursued lengthy discussions about a London production. It went to London's Comedy Theatre on January 30, 1958, with Kim Stanley as Maggie. *Theatre Arts*, June 1955. *General Collections, Library of Congress.*

Miller worked regularly, both in New York and London, on occasion copresenting plays with Stevens in New York.

That men of this caliber worked so well and closely with the relative newcomer Stevens is strong testimony to the rapid development of Stevens's stature in London as well as New York.

Stevens's association with London's theatre world started very shortly after he began his work as a producer on Broadway. Stevens was an active investor in a number of theatre productions in New York even before he presented *Twelfth Night* in 1949. He invested in a presentation by Alfred de Liagre, Jr., a well-known Broadway producer, of an adaptation by Maurice Valency of *The Madwoman of Chaillot* by Jean Giraudoux. This may have been Stevens's first connection with the writer, whom he so well regarded. The play opened at New York's Belasco Theatre in December 1948. Subsequently, de Liagre, who

Phyllis Neilson-Terry, Margaret Leighton, and Eric Portman in *Table Number Seven*, one of the two plays comprising *Separate Tables*. Coproduced in New York by the Producers' Theatre, it opened October 25, 1956, at the Music Box. World Telegram and Sun *Collection, Prints and Photographs Division, Library of Congress*

Stevens was associated with the American production of two plays by Terence Rattigan—*Separate Tables* and, just one week later, his comedy, *The Sleeping Prince*. Here we see Eric Portman and Margaret Leighton in *Separate Tables*. Poster. *Roger L. Stevens Collection, Music Division, Library of Congress.*

became a long-time associate of Stevens, brought his *Madwoman* production to London in conjunction with the British producer Bernard Delfont, opening at Gilbert Miller's St. James Theatre on February 15, 1951. Stevens accompanied de Liagre on a trip to London at about this time and was invited by Binkie Beaumont to a party at Beaumont's home. It is not clear whether this was Stevens's first meeting with Beaumont, but it was not very long thereafter that the two began to communicate regularly, beginning a complex working relationship about theatre production in New York and London. Beaumont was by no means Stevens's only producing partner in West End activities. But he certainly was the most important, at least in the 1950s.

In July 1953, Stevens and Beaumont were exchanging letters about a new play by S. N. Behrman, formerly a member, originally a founding member, of the Playwrights' Company. At this time, Stevens, Whitehead, and Dowling were organizing the new producing entity, Producers' Theatre, and apparently were considering the new Behrman play for its first venture. The play, then titled *Duveen*, was based on Behrman's *New Yorker* profiles on Duveen, a well-known art dealer of the time with offices in New York. The correspondence makes clear that, even in this still early point in Stevens's producing career, the highly experienced Beaumont was committing time and thought to substantive discussions about play production with the relative newcomer. The letters about *Duveen* outline the efforts of both men to get Robert Morley for the lead. Beaumont felt that the play would be a splendid vehicle for Morley in London and New York, as, apparently, did Stevens, and the two men pursued the idea of production both in New York and London with Morley in mind.

Although Morley did not appear to be interested, efforts to sign him continued, but in the meantime there were also discussions with a view to getting Charles Laughton. Ralph Richardson and Alec Guinness were also mentioned as possibilities. The letters exemplify a working relationship moored in efforts to ensure a quality production, artists of the very first water coming under consideration.

Ultimately, neither Stevens nor Beaumont produced the play, which was presented under the title *Lord Pengo* with Charles Boyer in the lead in New York at the Royale Theatre, beginning November 19, 1962; but it was never presented in London.

At about this time, there was mention in the Stevens/Beaumont correspondence of the possibility of a production of Giraudoux's *Ondine*, the tragic fantasy about the love of a water sprite for a human. A version from the Theatre National de Belgique had been presented in July 1953 at the Lyric Theatre Hammersmith in London by Beaumont's Tennent organization. Stevens was formulating an entirely new production. At this point, Audrey Hepburn who was eventually to star in the play in New York, was not being mentioned. Beaumont and Stevens exchanged communications about their interest in Mai Zetterling, a Swedish actress, for the role. At this early stage, Beaumont was thinking in terms of nonprofit presentation for a pro-

Roger Stevens was often associated with Gilbert Miller, a major producer who, like Stevens, had interests both in London and New York and, also like Stevens, was responsible for many quality productions of European and American plays. Miller is seen here with Audrey Hepburn and Michael Evans preparing for his presentation of *Gigi*. *Look*, October 31, 1051. *General Collections, Library of Congress.*

duction which might not have general appeal, at least not without a major star draw. But when Hepburn was signed for the role of the water sprite Ondine in New York, Beaumont appeared eager to have her take on the role in London. Hepburn did not choose to do that, and a London production was never achieved. *Ondine* opened at the 46th Street Theatre in New York on February 18, 1954, under the direction of Alfred Lunt, who was broadly given credit for a superb staging. The production did well as long as Hepburn remained, achieving 117 performances before she withdrew, following which the producers put up the closing notice.

During this same season, on May 26, 1954, Stevens wrote Beaumont expressing regret that Beaumont was not interested in bringing *In the Summer House* to London. Jane Bowles's play had achieved a critical success in New York, with Judith Anderson starring, presented by the Playwrights' Company with Oliver Smith at New York's Playhouse Theatre, beginning December 29, 1953. Beaumont did not appear to think it could achieve a London success. But Stevens apparently felt strongly about the high quality of the play and made an effort to bring Beaumont around.

Stevens made a similar effort the following year, corresponding with Beaumont about whether Peggy Ashcroft might consider playing the lead in Arthur Laurents's new play, *A Clearing in the Woods*. The hope was that Ashcroft might do it in London or New York, or both. Eventually, Ashcroft declined, and a London production did not materialize. However, the play opened in New York on January 10, 1957, at the Belasco Theatre, presented by Stevens and Oliver Smith, with Kim Stanley in the lead. It was a critical success, but a financial failure.

The American-born T. S. Eliot and the British writer Christopher Fry were very likely the most eminent writers of poetic works active in London at midcentury. Stevens was interested in the work of both men. At about the time that Stevens was presenting *Ondine* in New York, he was working with the British producer Henry Sherek in presenting T. S. Eliot's new comedy, *The Confidential Clerk*, to New York. The play had achieved a fair success in London, produced by Sherek, opening at the Lyric Theatre on September 16, 1953, subsequently transferring to the Duke of York's for a total of 259 performances. In New York, the play was a very early production of the new Producers' Theatre entity, opening at the Morosco Theatre, one of the City Playhouses group, on February 11, 1954, for a run of 117 performances. This production brought a great star, Ina Claire, back to the New York stage. She was famed for her brilliance in high comedy and had been much sought after for a return to the stage. She chose the Eliot play. While it had a run of almost three months, it was not a success, but is one more instance of the level on which Stevens worked.

Later in 1954, on August 4, Samuel Taylor's *Sabrina Fair* opened at London's Palace Theatre, presented by Emile Littler and Peter Daubeny for a run of 149 performances. Taylor was one of the finest writers of American comedy of the time. This staging was the first instance of a London production of a play which had been presented earlier in New York through one of the producing entities with which Stevens was connected. In New York, it had opened at the National Theatre

Roger Stevens coproduced Arthur Laurents's *A Clearing in the Woods* (starring Kim Stanley) with Oliver Smith. Smith was associated in other instances with Stevens—as scenic designer for other Stevens productions and as a member of the committee for the National Cultural Center, later the Kennedy Center. *Van Damm Photographs, Music Division, Library of Congress.*

under the Playwrights' Company on November 11, 1953, giving 318 performances. It was not the success in London that it was in New York.

Similarly Maxwell Anderson's *The Bad Seed*, which had achieved success in New York, did not do well in London. The play shocked many by its rendering of the story of a child murderess whose deeds, in the stage version, are never discovered or punished. It was the initial presentation in London under H. M. Tennent's auspices of a production which had originated with one of Stevens's producing entities, in this case the Playwrights' Company, of which Anderson was a founding member. The play had achieved 334 performances in New York, opening at the 46th Street Theatre on December 4, 1954. After its opening in New York, Beaumont informed Stevens of his interest in the play, and Stevens apparently held the property for Beaumont until Beaumont had had a chance to read the script. Robert Dowling took the script to Beaumont in London, and Beaumont expressed a desire to mount a production in the very near term. It opened under H. M. Tennent at the Aldwych Theatre in London on April 14, 1955, directed by Frith Banbury; but it achieved only 195 performances.

In May 26, 1954, Stevens wrote Beaumont about his interest in Fry's play, *The Dark Is Light Enough*, noting that Whitehead, a partner in the Producers' Theatre, was not enthusiastic about the play, that it would be advisable then to do it under the Playwrights' Company. The play was the first H. M. Tennent production done in New York through any of the groups with which Stevens was connected. It had done well under Beaumont, starring Edith Evans, with direction by Peter Brook, opening at the Aldwych Theatre on April 30, 1954, for a run of 243 performances. In New York, Stevens presented it with Katherine Cornell at the ANTA Theatre, opening on February 23, 1955, with Cornell as a suffering, high-minded aristocrat in the country in midnineteenth-century Austria, and Tyrone Power as an unprincipled scoundrel. Oliver Messel designed the production, as he did in London. But the play closed after sixty-nine performances.

The following year, in a letter dated May 23, 1956, Stevens wrote Beaumont asking an opinion as soon as possible about a translation by Fry of a Giraudoux play, *Pour Lucrece*. Beaumont wrote the following week that Lilli Palmer thought it a masterpiece and was anxious to do it. The play had two major roles for actresses—one, Lucile, representing good; the other, Paola, embodying evil. Deborah Kerr apparently also promised to read the script. This began a long road to production, both in London and New York, of a presentation which came to be called *Duel of Angels*.

At some point, Vivien Leigh came into the discussion. On April 11, 1957, Beaumont advised Stevens that he had not yet heard from Leigh with a decision as to which part she wanted to play or when, but that Peter Brook, apparently intended at the time as director, was in constant touch with her. In June, Beaumont wrote Stevens that he was going to meet with Laurence Olivier and Cecil Tennant to discuss pro-

Arthur Laurents wrote the book for *West Side Story*. It was Laurents who made the call to London to Roger Stevens when the show's artistic group was in despair, fearing that the production would not happen. But Stevens wasted no time in coming through with support. *Look*, September 1, 1959. *Prints and Photographs Division, Library of Congress.*

Sheet music for "Tonight" from *West Side Story*. The production became one of the classics of American musical theatre. *Music Division, Library of Congress*

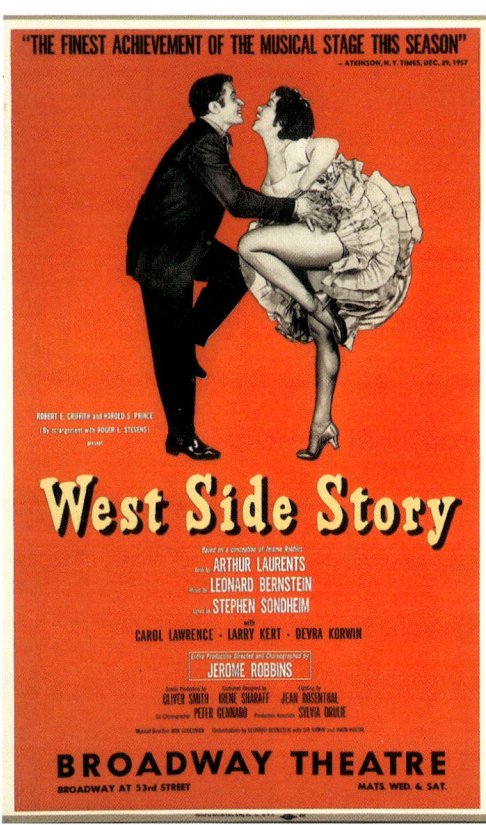

The Broadway production of *West Side Story*, with sets designed by Oliver Smith. Color poster. *Roger L. Stevens Collection, Music Division, Library of Congress.*

A jubilant Leonard Bernstein celebrates the success of his *West Side Story* in August 1957 in front of the marquee of Washington's National Theatre, where the show had its world premiere—thanks in great part to Roger Stevens—before going on to New York. *Leonard Bernstein Collection, Music Division, Library of Congress.*

Rehearsing *West Side Story*. Ken LeRoy as leader of the Sharks, Chita Rivera as his girl. Jerome Robbins, choreographer and director, is credited with having had the inspiration for a musical based on *Romeo and Juliet*. *World Telegram and Sun Collection, Prints and Photographs Division, Library of Congress.*

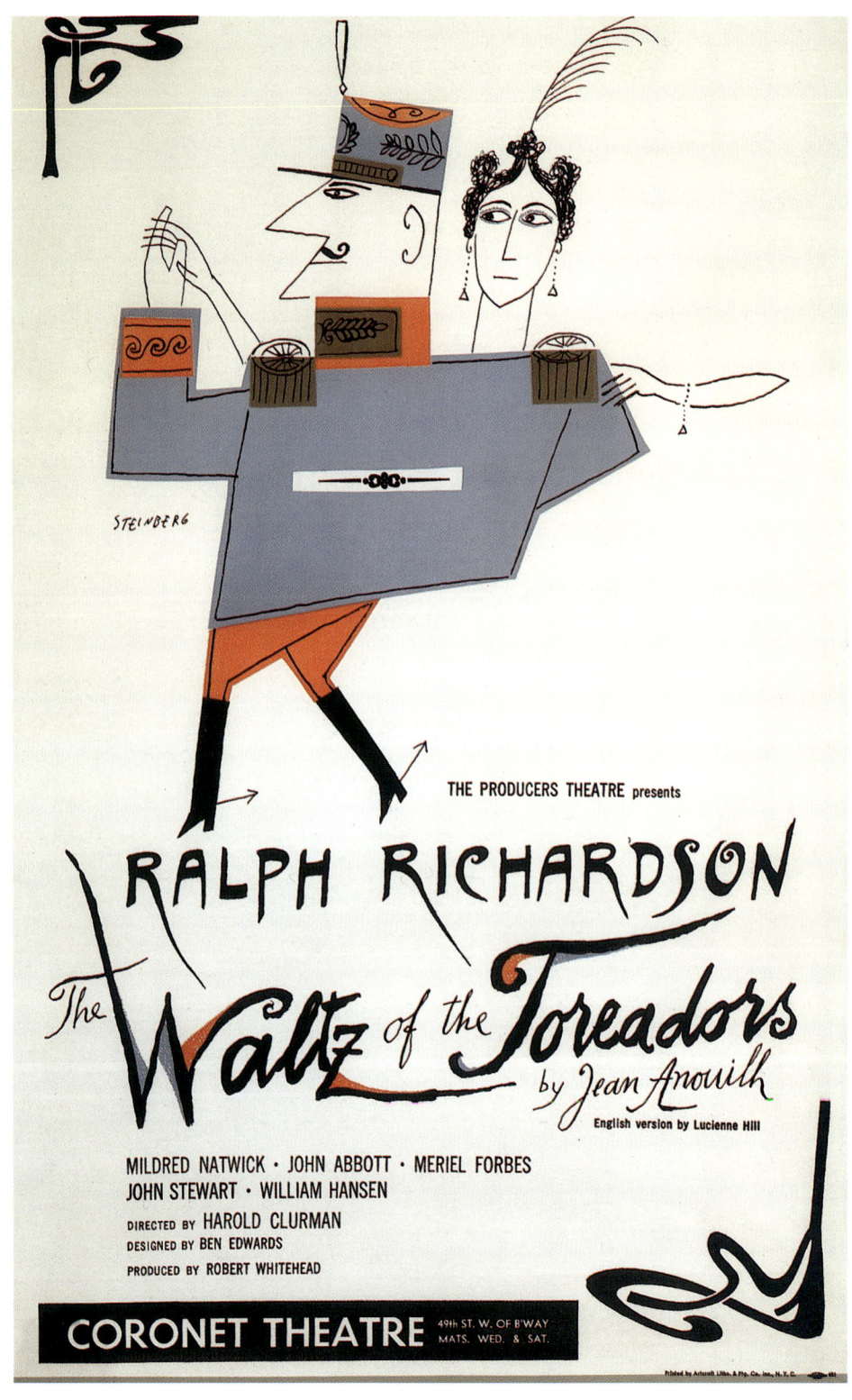

Waltz of the Toreadors was one of Jean Anouilh's first successes in New York, and the first of the French playwright's works with which Stevens was associated. Ralph Richardson was General St. Pe. Color poster. *Roger L. Stevens Collection, Music Division, Library of Congress.*

In 1954, Roger Stevens told director Albert Marre that he would see to the production of a play of Marre's choosing. The next year, Marre brought him a script for *Time Remembered*, which Stevens produced, casting Richard Burton and Susan Strasberg. *Van Damm Photographs, Music Division, Library of Congress.*

Time Remembered was a critical success. The cast included Helen Hayes (center) and Susan Strasberg (left). *Van Damm Photographs, Music Division, Library of Congress.*

Time Remembered was an expensive and lavish production, with Oliver Smith sets that were deemed especially beautiful. *Van Damm Photographs, Music Division, Library of Congress.*

ducing *Pour Lucrece*. In August, Beaumont wrote that Kerr would like to do the play, at least in London, if she were available. But her film contract commitments were a concern.

Peter Brook may by that time have withdrawn from the Giraudoux plans, because in September Beaumont was writing Stevens that he had given a script to Peter Glenville, who apparently did not care much for the casting plans. Beaumont expressed his intention, having talked to Leigh, to approach Jean-Louis Barrault, who eventually did direct in London. In October, there still was no commitment from Kerr, who eventually withdrew. Late in 1957, Stevens had given copies of the script to Julie Harris and Irene Worth, but in late December, Beaumont wrote that Claire Bloom was fairly definite for Lucile. The play opened as *Duel of Angels* at the Apollo Theatre in London on April 24, 1958, running for 251 performances. The New York production opened on April 19, 1960, at the Helen Hayes, formerly the Fulton Theatre, presented by Stevens and Sol Hurok, with Leigh as Paola and Mary Ure as Lucile. It had only fifty-one performances.

On June 7, 1957, Beaumont reported to Stevens that Alfred Lunt and Lynn Fontanne had definitely agreed to the do the play by the Swiss playwright, Friedrich Duerrenmatt, which was at that time being called *The Old Lady's Visit*, a title which the Lunts refused to accept. The Lunts had earlier refused the play. They went to London to prepare for the production of *The Great Sebastians*, but the Swiss play came under discussion. Finally, the Lunts decided not to do *Sebastian*, but to take on what came to be called *The Visit*. The script was something of a departure for the Lunts, having to do with a woman's ultimate and devastating revenge on a former lover by having him killed by his townsfolk in return for much needed economic aid for the town that the now wealthy old woman could furnish. Peter Brook was scheduled to direct this also. But the Lunts would go no further than the verbal commitment until they could know the outcome of a session scheduled for later in the year in Paris with the author, Brook, and Maurice Valency, who was doing the adaptation. Work continued on the script for some time. Rehearsals were scheduled for November, with an opening in Brighton planned for Christmas Eve. On December 30, Beaumont wrote Stevens that the premiere in Brighton had proved a shock to an audience that had seemed to expect a light comedy. (Since the advertisements for the play apparently advertised it as such, that should not have been surprising.) The play did not come into London then as had been planned. Instead the Lunts took the play to New York where, on May 5, 1958, under the auspices of the Producers' Theatre, it inaugurated the Lunt-Fontanne Theatre, which City Investing had rebuilt from the Globe Theatre in the Times Square area. The play was not successful in New York, nor eventually in London, when the Lunts returned to England with it in 1960. But Stevens once again was deeply involved with the realization of a production that was considered by many to have been a singularly powerful event and theatre of the finest kind.

Facing page:
Roger Stevens acquired the American production rights to *The Visit* on reading the script. First refused by the Lunts, he worked to put on a masterful production which was one of the great moments in midcentury theater in New York. Here we see the Alfred Lunt character being attacked. *Van Damm Photographs, Music Division, Library of Congress.*

City Investing Co., with which Stevens and Robert Dowling were associated, created one of New York's loveliest and most elegant playhouses in the completely renovated Lunt-Fontanne Theatre. Formerly the Globe (its facade is seen here), it had been home to productions of Charles Dillingham, one of the great musical theatre producers of the early twentieth century. *Theatre Arts*, May 1958. *General Collections. Library of Congress.*

Lynn Fontanne, Alfred Lunt, and Helen Hayes in front of the Lunt-Fontanne Theatre in New York. Across the street is the Helen Hayes Theatre, at which, in 1958, Miss Hayes appeared in the Producers' Theatre presentation of Eugene O'Neill's *A Touch of the Poet*. World Telegram and Sun *Collection, Prints and Photographs Division, Library of Congress.*

"Oh, the towering feeling just to be on the street where you live" is the caption on the drawing being given to Alfred Lunt and Lynn Fontanne by Helen Hayes. The Hayes and newly renamed Lunt-Fontanne theatres faced one another on New York's West 46th Street. World Telegram and Sun *Collection, Prints and Photographs Division, Library of Congress.*

Alfred Lunt and Lynn Fontanne in Maurice Valency's adaptation of Friedrich Duerrenmatt's play *The Visit*. Behind them are John Wyse and Eric Porter. Lunt as Anton Schill is the intended victim of the deadly demand Claire Zachanassian makes on his townspeople. World Telegram and Sun *Collection, Prints and Photographs Division, Library of Congress.*

Caricature of the British director, Peter Brook, by David Low. Through his direction of productions such as Duerrenmatt's *The Physicist* and *The Visit*, Brook was one of the many fine theatre artists with whom Stevens was associated. *Swann Collection, Prints and Photographs Division, Library of Congress.*

Teo Otto's scenic designs for London and this New York production of *The Visit* were a much simplified version of the sets he created for earlier presentations of the play on the Continent. Color poster. *Roger L. Stevens Collection, Music Division, Library of Congress.*

Frederick Brisson, Roger Stevens, and Jayne Meadows, who starred with Walter Slezak in *The Gazebo*, which was coproduced by the Playwrights' Company and Brisson in 1958. Brisson was associated with Stevens in other productions, including Samuel Taylor's *First Love*. Directed by Alfred Lunt, it opened in New York on December 25, 1961. *Roger L. Stevens Collection, Music Division, Library of Congress.*

In 1955, Emile Littler, who had been one of the London producers of *Sabrina Fair*, wrote Stevens about a project which was conceived to be a theatre club in London which could be used for the presentation of plays that might be considered problematic by London's Lord Chamberlain, who reviewed plays for London production. Eventually, the Comedy Theatre in London housed at least two productions of a new producing entity called the New Watergate Club, in which Beaumont was involved. The unit produced the London premieres of Robert Anderson's *Tea and Sympathy* and Tennessee Williams's *Cat on a Hot Tin Roof,* both of which had been produced in New York through the Playwrights' Company, the first in 1953, the second in 1955. There had been talk that Deborah Kerr might repeat her role in the London production of *Tea and Sympathy* and of trying alternatively to get Ingrid Bergman. But eventually Elizabeth Sellars played Kerr's role in a production which opened April 27, 1957, for 173 performances.

Kim Stanley went to London for *Cat on a Hot Tin Roof* to play Maggie, a performance which Beaumont thought very fine. Beaumont

Cornelia Otis Skinner, Dolores Hart, and Cyril Ritchard walking by New York's Music Box Theatre. They were in the cast of *The Pleasure of His Company*, coproduced by the Playwrights' Company. In 1959, it was transferred to that theatre. World Telegram and Sun *Collection, Prints and Photographs Division, Library of Congress.*

wrote Stevens that Paul Scofield had turned down the offer to play Brick, apparently feeling that Maggie and Big Daddy, played in London by Leo McKern, were the big roles. The production opened under Peter Hall's direction on January 30, 1958, for 132 performances.

One of Stevens's solid financial successes, both critically and financially, in New York was *The Pleasure of His Company*, written by Samuel Taylor with Cornelia Otis Skinner. It was produced by Frederick Brisson and the Playwrights' Company at the Longacre Theatre, opening on October 20, 1958, and achieving a run of 474 performances. In the interests of a London production, Beaumont wrote to Stevens, mentioning several possibilities for the lead role of Biddeford "Pogo" Poole which Cyril Ritchard had originated in New York. Beaumont apparently had been quite active in investigating production possibilities. He had been in contact with John Gielgud, who was not interested in performing or directing. Beaumont put forward David Niven and George Sanders for the role, speculated about the availability of Robert Morley, and noted that Brisson had mentioned Ray Milland. When Nigel Patrick's name came up, Stevens, Brisson, and Taylor were highly supportive of Patrick's both directing and starring. The play opened at the Haymarket Theatre in London on April 23, 1959, and ran for 403 performances, only seventy-one short of the New York run.

With the death of Philip Barry in 1949, S. N. Behrman and Samuel Taylor were perhaps the best-known American dramatists writing civilized, or high, comedy. In the course of his career, Stevens presented a number of plays in this genre, American and European, including work by Somerset Maugham, William Douglas Home, and more recently A. R. Gurney and Enid Bagnold. After 1965, Stevens was away from theatre production for a few years, attending to his concerns in Washington with the National Cultural Center, and the National Endowment for the Arts. One of his very last productions before he began to devote full time to his Washington-based concerns was a presentation in London of Enid Bagnold's *The Chinese Prime Minister*, which he had presented in New York on January 2, 1964, then taken it

Cornelia Otis Skinner and Cyril Ritchard in *The Pleasure of His Company*, which opened on October 22, 1958, in New York. Skinner coauthored the play with Samuel Taylor, and Ritchard directed. World Telegram and Sun *Collection, Prints and Photographs Division, Library of Congress.*

The director and star of *The Pleasure of His Company* were the same, both in New York and London: Cyril Ritchard in New York, Nigel Patrick as "Pogo" in London, where the play opened on April 23, 1959, at the Haymarket Theatre for a run of 403 performances, almost as many as in New York. *Van Damm Photographs, Music Division, Library of Congress.*

to London's Globe Theatre on May 20, 1965, with Edith Evans in the role which Margaret Leighton had created in New York. Bagnold was one of the finest writers of thoughtful and civilized comedy in mid-century.

Roger L. Stevens did a great deal over the years to promote many, many plays he thought represented something fine in the theatre. While some were not successful commercially, Stevens gave the public a rare opportunity, if they cared to take advantage of it, to see remarkable productions. He joins the thin ranks of those producers in our theatre history who had a concern with giving the public the very best.

Roger Stevens
The Arts Endowment Years—
The Theatre Program

Ruth Mayleas

By November 1965, and before the arrival of major program staff, the National Endowment for the Arts had already marked its adventurous creative course. The agency was led by Roger Stevens, who had been Special Assistant to Pres. Lyndon Johnson, and who was subsequently appointed Chairman of the National Council on the Arts and of the newly created—in September 1965—National Endowment for the Arts. A fortuitous combination of circumstances had made this remarkable man—who combined what he called "a sort of knack I had of making deals" with an acute artistic sensibility, and in particular a reverence for the written and spoken word—leader of this bold and long-awaited experiment in government support of the arts. Some might have expected a foundation or university president, perhaps a politician, maybe even an artist, to be chosen to be the first leader of the Arts Endowment. Instead, the president chose a prominent Democrat with a background in real estate and commercial theatre producing for the job. And weren't we—the country, the arts community, and Roger's Arts Endowment colleagues who worked with him in those heady early days—lucky in that choice. In the fall of 1965 Roger Stevens said, "We cannot merely buy and sell culture in the marketplace; it must be fought for, earned, and won. The Federal Government, then, has a commitment and a clear responsibility toward this end." This was not empty rhetoric; it was a true statement of belief, and it was carried out.

The National Council on the Arts had met several times since its establishment in 1964, but the programs initiated at the historic November 1965 meeting represented the first actual allocation of funds for the Endowment's support of the arts. Included were: $755,000 earmarked for grants to creative artists in various fields; operational and touring grants to save a national treasure, American Ballet Theatre; a housing project to provide low-rental housing and studios to artists; the Laboratory Theatre Project, which combined instructional and artistic objectives, using funds from the far-better-endowed Office of Education, to enable theatre companies to perform for high school students during the day and play to adult paying audiences in the evening; and the Playwrights Experimental Theatre project, which provided funds for enhancing the production values of new

Copyright © Ruth Mayleas, 2001.

Anita Loos adapted *Chéri* from two works by Colette—*Chéri* and *The Last of Chéri*. Kim Stanley was Lea, the older woman with whom the nineteen-year-old Chéri, played by the German Horst Buchholz, falls in love. Both received enthusiastic notices. Color poster. *Peggy Clark Collection, Music Division, Library of Congress.*

Chéri was presented by the Playwrights' Company and Robert Lewis on October 12, 1959, at the Morosco Theatre in New York, starring Kim Stanley and Horst Buchholz. Lewis, who directed, also had *Brigadoon, Teahouse of the August Moon,* and *Witness for the Prosecution* among his credits. *Van Damm Photographs, Music Division, Library of Congress.*

Chéri opened to positive critical response in Washington at the National Theatre on September 21, 1958, before going to New York. The production, with ten scenes, was lavish, Miles White's costumes receiving considerable comment. *Van Damm Photographs, Music Division, Library of Congress.*

works of literary merit to be chosen and presented by regional and university theatres.

Support for the creative artist was the thread that ran through these varied initiatives, the tie that bound them programmatically and vividly marked Roger Stevens's and the new agency's commitment to creativity and excellence. It was also no accident that the National Council members present at that meeting—including such major artistic figures as Rene d'Harnoncourt, Ralph Ellison, Agnes de Mille, Paul Engle, and Oliver Smith—were Stevens's choices.

Is timing everything? Or rather, is being in the right place at the right time everything? In this case the time was the mid-sixties and the place was the American National Theatre and Academy (ANTA)— of which Roger Stevens was treasurer and I head of a department that dealt with the then-emerging nonprofit professional regional theatre. Thus I had the great good fortune to be appointed the first director of the Theatre Program of the National Endowment for the Arts, a daunting challenge indeed to work with a man who had been the most creative and wide- ranging theatre producer in New York.

Juno was presented by the Playwrights' Company with Oliver Smith and Oliver Rea. Agnes de Mille choreographed the show, and Jose Ferrer directed. Jean Stapleton and Sada Thompson were noteworthy in the cast. *Van Damm Photographs, Music Division, Library of Congress.*

Richard Rodgers, Oscar Hammerstein II, Mary Martin, Russell Crouse, and Howard Lindsay were responsible for *The Sound of Music*, which was a great success at the Lunt-Fontanne Theatre, renovated by City Investing Inc., one of Stevens's many associations. World Telegram and Sun *Collection, Prints and Photographs Division, Library of Congress*.

Stevens had entered the Broadway theatre at a time of expanding productivity, when its horizons were broadening. He also entered it as a wealthy man who could take a long chance on plays deemed noncommercial, whose prospects of achieving financial success were small. In addition to the many distinguished American writers whose works he produced, Stevens was responsible for bringing to this country works by such European luminaries as Giraudoux, Anouilh, and Duerrenmatt, and for the introduction of Harold Pinter to Broadway audiences. The job was daunting as well because of actual and potential Congressional opposition and extreme budgetary constraints—2.5 million dollars in program funds in fiscal 1966. At that time I knew Stevens only slightly and was somewhat intimidated by his austere presence as we occasionally rode the narrow elevator at 1545 Broadway to the ANTA offices. Nonetheless, never one to waste words, Roger expended all of fifteen minutes on my job interview. The next thing I knew I was in Washington, arriving in the middle of a snowstorm (which closed all government offices) in late January 1966, working for and with Stevens to carry out the early theatre projects

Roland Culver and Jessica Tandy in Peter Shaffer's *Five Finger Exercise*. Directed by John Gielgud, the play, seen first in London, was one the many points of contact between Stevens and Hugh Beaumont of the British producing firm, H. M. Tennent Ltd. It opened in New York December 2, 1959. World Telegram and Sun *Collection, Prints and Photographs Division, Library of Congress*

The Best Man was the last production of the Playwrights' Company and it featured Melvyn Douglas and Frank Lovejoy. Gore Vidal's play about an American presidential nominating convention was a great success in New York's 1959-1960 theatre season, opening at the Morosco Theatre on March 31, 1960. *Life*, April 25, 1960. *General Collections, Library of Congress.*

outlined and approved at that November Council meeting and develop new ones. Those first projects in theatre and dance (I was for a short time involved in the administration of the Dance Program as well)—the Laboratory Theatre Project, the Playwrights Experimental Theatre, the rescuing of American Ballet Theatre, and commissions to major choreographers—were remarkable for their originality, their collaboration with other agencies, and above all for their focus on the artist and the stimulation of new creative work.

Because Endowment budget projections for the next fiscal years were minuscule and the exposure of young people to live theatre of high literary and performance quality was an unarguably beneficial educational goal, Stevens was successful in persuading the Office of Education to provide large infusions of funds, matched by much smaller Arts Endowment monies, to three (two new, one preexisting) theatre companies in New Orleans, Los Angeles, and Providence, Rhode Island. The injection of what were then considered sizeable funds to Trinity Square Repertory Theatre, a fledgling, though brilliantly led group in Providence, enabled it to become one of the most innovative theatres in the country; to this day—thirty-four years later—it continues the school program begun in 1967, still called Project Discovery.

Barry Nelson and Barbara Bel Geddes in *Mary, Mary*, one of the major comedy successes of the 1960s. Stevens was the presenter. Written by Jean Kerr, the play opened at the Helen Hayes Theatre on March 8, 1961. World Telegram and Sun *Collection, Prints and Photographs Division, Library of Congress.*

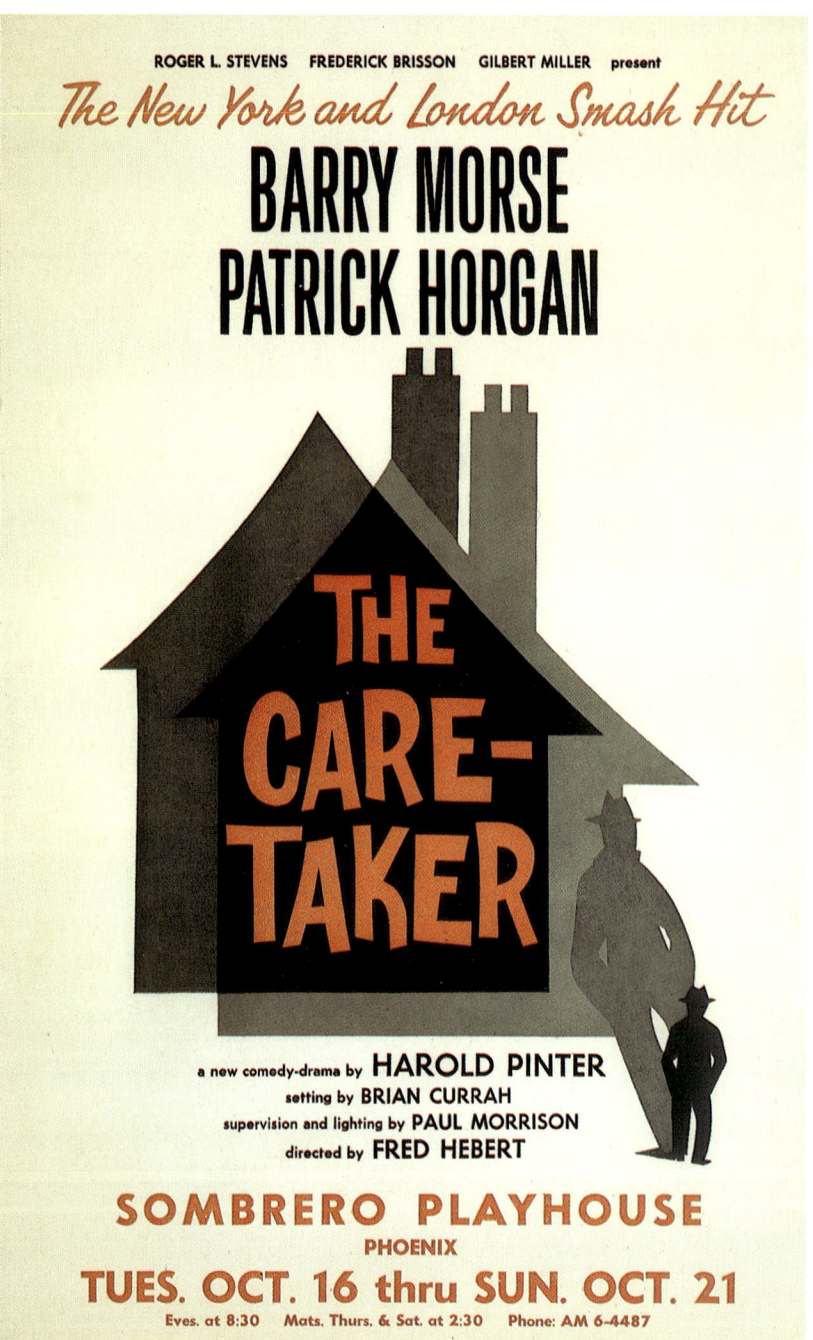

With Frederick Brisson and Gilbert Miller, Roger Stevens presented the American premiere of Harold Pinter's *The Caretaker* on October 4, 1961, at New York's Lyceum Theatre. With Peter Hall, Stevens also presented Pinter's *The Homecoming* at the Aldywch Theatre in London beginning June 3, 1965. Color poster. *Roger L. Stevens Collection, Music Division, Library of Congress.*

Roger's passion for playwrights and the discovery of new work, inspired the Playwrights Experimental Theatre, which gave matching grants to five regional and university theatres for production enhancement of new plays that had been submitted by the theatres and subsequently selected by a jury. Of the five plays, two were eventually produced on Broadway, the most notable being *The Great White Hope*, which put its producer, Arena Stage, on the national map and, most importantly, marked a major change in the flow of new dramatic work: *from* regional theatres and other nonprofits *to* Broadway, instead of the preexisting reverse. That pattern continues to this day and has indeed changed the face of the American theatre. This pro-

Arthur Kopit's *Oh Dad, Poor Dad, Mamma's Hung You in the Closet and I'm Feelin' So Sad*, Jerome Robbins, director, opened at New York's Morosco Theatre on August 27, 1963. The play was coproduced by Stevens. World Telegram and Sun *Collection, Prints and Photographs Division, Library of Congress.*

gram of direct support for new plays was in the next year fed into an expanded grant program to regional and other nonprofit theatres whose guidelines encouraged proposals for new play development and production.

Another highly experimental initiative, much remarked upon at the time, was the American Theatre Laboratory, involving all categories of performing arts. The project provided for the setting up of a lab—physically, a large flexible space—in New York City for musicians, choreographers, actors, writers, and dancers to work under the direction of choreographer/director Jerome Robbins. Criticized for its large expenditure (almost three hundred thousand dollars) for one artist,

Roger Stevens was eager to see Gore Vidal follow up on his success with *The Best Man*. Vidal decided to adapt Duerrenmatt's *Romulus der Grosse*, about the last Roman emperor, Romulus Augustulus. Stevens liked the idea of a fantastic look at the fall of the Roman Empire and produced it. Color poster. *Peggy Clark Collection, Music Division, Library of Congress.*

Alan Webb and Margaret Leighton in *The Chinese Prime Minister* by Enid Bagnold, one of the finest British writers of her time. Stevens presented it in New York before giving the play its first production in London. The play opened in New York on January 2, 1964, at the Royale Theatre. World Telegram and Sun *Collection. Prints and Photographs Division, Library of Congress.*

however gifted, to develop projects as he wished, with no predefined outcomes, it could be said to be a quintessential Stevens grant: daring and exploratory—a testament to Stevens's belief in talented artists and the creative spirit.

A more modest grant to help establish the Theatre Development Fund also received some criticism, though this time from the nonprofit theatre world. Though TDF's concept was unusual, providing subsidy in the form of ticket price support for the production on Broadway of seemingly noncommercial plays of literary merit—its purpose to stimulate creativity and experimentation on Broadway—the organization's commercial focus made it questionable to the nonprofit world. Today TDF stands as a well-established part of the New York theatre community and has expanded its programs to many facets of the performing arts, including the nonprofit sector.

The National Endowment's birth in 1965 coincided with a burst of activity and accelerated growth in the nonprofit professional theatre in New York and regionally. The Alley Theatre in Houston had been founded in 1947, Arena Stage in Washington in 1950, the Milwaukee Rep in 1954, the Seattle Rep and the Guthrie in Minneapolis in 1963, the latter with great fanfare and distinguished actors (Hume Cronyn and Jessica Tandy led the list) in its first repertory company. Thus, the early Stevens efforts to target artists, and particularly playwrights, was joined by an effort to address the potential and the needs of this decentralized professional theatre on a broad scale. It was also important to better acquaint Council and staff with this new universe, to give them first-hand exposure to what was going on theatrically around the country. I have a distinct memory (though I can't recall the date) of taking part in a whirlwind trip to Boston with Roger, Council member Gregory Peck, and several others to see matinee and evening performances, back to back, at the Charles Playhouse and the Theatre Company of Boston. With no time for dinner, a hungry group ended up in Roger's suite at the Ritz enjoying a midnight room service supper. Traveling with Roger was often fun—as well as hard work.

During the first four years, these two theatres and approximately thirty others were participants in the Arts Endowment's first program, launched in fiscal 1967, of direct support to regional theatres for creative projects. It was followed a year later, in fiscal 1968, by a similar nationwide effort—the first such endeavor by any funding agency, public or private—for experimental theatres and workshops which had also proliferated around the country as well as in New York. Both programs had advisory panels, which I recall Stevens agreeing to with some slight reluctance—the producer confident of his own taste and instincts confronting his more cautious bureaucratic staff which seeks both advice and the protection afforded by the recommendation of experts. (It was many years later that we were to learn, sadly, that panels and experts are no defense against an inflamed legislature or public or press.) But even back then, panels were not new to the young Arts Endowment. In the field of dance, before any staff had been engaged, Council member Agnes de Mille formed a panel of luminaries in ballet and contemporary dance, making possible the heretofore mentioned saving of American Ballet Theatre and the first choreographer commissions which included grants to Merce Cunningham, José Limon, and Paul Taylor.

The $25,000 top on grants to regional theatres was amplified in special cases to take advantage of matching grants from outside sources that made possible large-scale support to the new American Conservatory Theatre, enabling it to move from Pittsburgh to San Francisco (this project occasioned another whirlwind trip, to San Francisco, this time to meet with a potential private donor); special assistance to Joseph Papp's New York Shakespeare Festival, which was building an extraordinary producing center in the former Astor Library on Lafayette Street; and assistance to the remarkable and long-lived APA-Phoenix with its eclectic repertory.

Those early programs in all fields told the story. They focused entirely on the artist, from choreographer commissions to sabbaticals

The great comedy success *Mary, Mary* was not Stevens's only association with the playwright Jean Kerr. He presented her play *Poor Richard* on December 2, 1964, at the Helen Hayes Theatre in New York and worked with her and her husband, critic and writer Walter Kerr, who together wrote the book for the 1958 musical *Goldilocks*. Color poster. *Roger L. Stevens Collection, Music Division, Library of Congress.*

for artists teaching in educational institutions, to supplemental income for creative writers and visual artists, to moderate-cost housing for artists. In the Theatre Program in particular, Stevens's focus was on artistic development, whether through direct grants to playwrights or to institutions for artistic purposes. The early guidelines to nonprofit theatres singled out artistic purposes, and the panels were encouraged to regard the artistic quality of the institution as the key criterion.

Roger Stevens was a striking public figure and much has been written about his exploits in real estate and his achievements at the

Kennedy Center. But I believe that there has been too little attention given to his equally remarkable record as the first chairman of the National Endowment for the Arts. Leadership of the agency in those early years was a delicate and demanding task, requiring connections in high places, political savvy, an understanding of the existing support structure of the arts, and a comprehension of the needs of the arts in a period of extraordinary artistic growth and expansion. Roger had these qualities in abundance.

Though I cannot speak for others, it was obvious to me that the early program staff—a distinguished group that included a well-known poet, Carolyn Kizer, and a leading museum curator, Henry Geldzahler—had both profound admiration and personal affection for their leader. A real humanity shone through that austere presence, as did artistic instincts and an ability to put dealmaking abilities to good use in tapping funds from other agencies and marrying unlikely program partners.

In the winter and early spring of 1969, after the Republicans had gained the White House, some of us had hoped that, regardless of political affiliation, Roger would be reappointed in recognition of the job so brilliantly begun. Alas, that was not to be. Roger's term was to expire in March 1969. When no word had come as to his reappointment, he walked from his office one springlike Saturday afternoon directly to the White House to ascertain his status. Senior staff often worked on Saturdays, so a number of us were on hand that day. I particularly remember Ana Steele, who was to retire from the Endowment as a deputy chairperson many years later—in 1998—being there. Later that afternoon Roger walked the short distance back from the White House to our offices at 1800 G Street, assembled us in his office, and gave us the sad word. Though the exact date and the details of who was present escape me, my feeling remains vivid to this day: it was one of profound sadness that we all shared that Roger could not remain as our leader. We would miss him—and we did.

In any case, the course that Roger Stevens set as the first Chairman of the Arts Endowment remained for many years as a standard for many of us. In particular, the principles of the Theatre Program, as marked out in those first four years, were followed for many more— and the American theatre is greatly in his debt.

The Man Behind Washington's Kennedy Center

Roger L. Stevens is an intensely practical visionary whose efforts have done a lot to turn the capital into a "good show town"

Tom Prideaux

When Roger L. Stevens' friends were planning a tribute to him at the Kennedy Center in Washington some time ago, they discussed what sort of gift to give. "Let's bring in a wagonload of hundred-dollar bills," said Abe Fortas, "and set it on fire."

But, even as a joke, they decided against it. For with Stevens' record as a prodigious spender and investor, it might have created an unfair image of a man with money to burn. Instead, at the end of a gala evening, they had Carol Channing sing "Hello, Roger" and gave him a plaque that called him an "unstoppable visionary."

Kennedy Center itself testifies that Stevens is a nonstop visionary. Since it opened in 1971 as both a memorial to President John F. Kennedy and a home for the performing arts, it has altered the quality of life in the nation's capital. More than 20 million sightseers have taken its free guided tours. Another 12 million have packed its theaters and concert halls, and attended its free educational programs. As a setting for social and semidiplomatic events, it generates a mood that is reassuring to foreign visitors. Between the acts of its performances, people enjoy sipping champagne on the long terrace, with its line of willow trees, its illuminated fountains, its lovely view of the Potomac; and they like promenading beneath its rows of international banners.

The Center is headed by a two-man team: Roger Stevens, chairman and prime mover, and Martin Feinstein, executive director. Feinstein is immensely effective at providing fine music and dance, while Stevens is mainly concerned with theatrical productions, many of which he fosters and nurses into existence specially for the Center. His operations are infuriating to some of his attackers. But beyond any doubt, if the city of Washington might once have been compared to the Sleeping Beauty, too deep in slumber to be aware of the performing arts, then Roger Stevens was the tall, blue-eyed prince whose kiss woke her up.

Born in Detroit in 1910, Stevens belatedly became something of a rags-to-riches case, but with an important difference. He took money for granted. His father, a well-to-do real estate broker, sent Roger to an Ivy-League prep school, Choate. Later Roger became fascinated by the

This article originally appeared in *Smithsonian* in January 1979.

manipulation of money, but he was never awed by it, any more than a chess player is awed by his chessmen. When the Depression struck his father, Roger canceled his enrollment at Harvard and entered the University of Michigan at Ann Arbor, to save money by living at home.

After a restless year, he quit the university and grabbed any jobs he could find: tending a gas station at $12 a week, polishing gears on a Ford assembly line. He also worked in a real estate office, earning nothing, learning a lot. Between times he camped in libraries, reading Fielding, Shaw, Shakespeare, Proust, Mann, Thomas Wolfe and Pirandello. The reading habit stuck with him.

Making a profit from real estate hunches

When the Depression abated, Stevens returned to real estate. He became a creative finagler. Seeing hidden values in failed hotels and office buildings, he gained control of them and then sold them at a profit until he had accumulated a nest egg of $50,000 at the age of 26 and was earning $25,000 a year. His greatest problem, he said, was finding other people who believed in his hunches.

In 1937 he found a true believer in attractive Christine Gesell, an Ann Arbor undergraduate whose uncle, Arnold, was the famous child psychologist. She married Stevens and they took off on a lavish six-month honeymoon around the world.

Back home, Stevens joined the Detroit Theater Guild, and walked into a new world where he could gamble on his taste and hunches—and meet exciting people. On a trip to New York he met a high-riding producer, Alfred de Liagre, Jr., and announced that he was ready to start his career by buying the old Belasco Theatre. De Liagre warned that theater-owning was risky, and Stevens ended up putting money into a new de Liagre production, *The Madwoman of Chaillot* by Jean Giraudoux, which won the 1949 Drama Critics Award as the year's best play and left Stevens incurably stagestruck.

He rushed *Twelfth Night* from an Ann Arbor festival to Broadway (it lost some $40,000), and backed Ibsen's *Peer Gynt,* and Barrie's *Peter Pan* with music by Leonard Bernstein (a financial hit).

Stevens' most arrestingly theatrical act, though unrelated to Broadway, took place in 1951. Creating a grand baroque pattern of deals and loans, he formed a syndicate to buy the Empire State Building for $51.5 million, the highest price ever paid for one edifice. The syndicate turned it over three years later at a profit of nearly $10 million.

Around Broadway Stevens was regarded as young Lochinvar out of the Midwest. He teamed up with Robert Whitehead to start a producing firm, and was named to the board of several high-minded theater groups: ANTA (American National Theatre and Academy), the Phoenix Theatre and, most impressive, the Playwrights' Company. This elite batch of dramatists, wanting to control the production of their own works (and those of a few chosen outsiders), picked Stevens to be their financial adviser—and also, they assured him, to give his

Roger Stevens was sworn in as Pres. Lyndon Baines Johnson's special assistant in the arts in May 1964, and was appointed chairman of the National Council on the Arts in February 1965. *Roger L. Stevens Collection, Music Division, Library of Congress.*

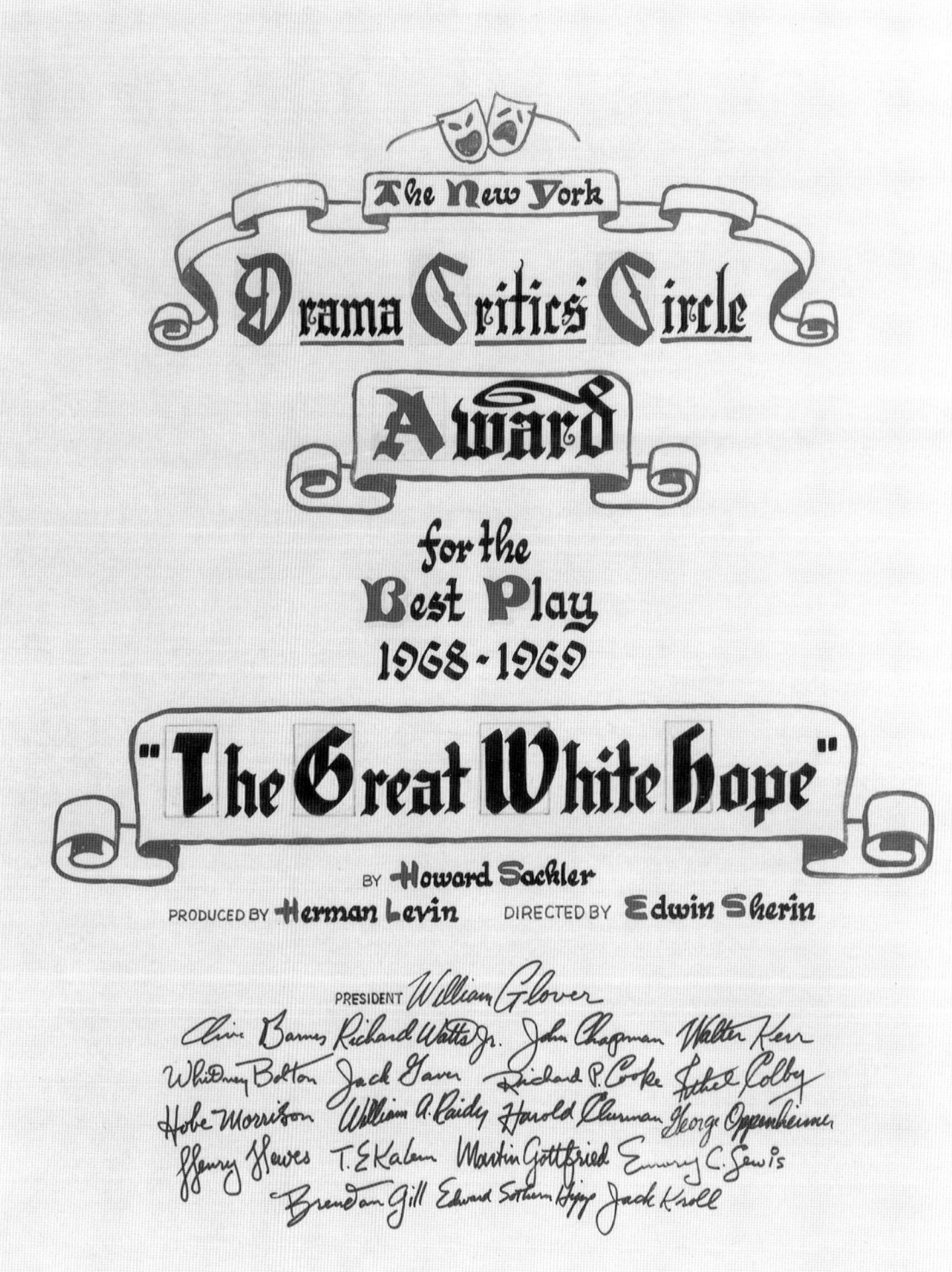

Shortly after the establishment of the National Endowment for the Arts, with Stevens as chairman, the NEA Theatre program established support grants for noteworthy plays. One of the great successes to come out of this was Howard Sackler's *The Great White Hope*. Award. *Lucy Kroll Collection, Manuscript Division, Library of Congress.*

In *The Great White Hope*, James Earl Jones was Jack Jefferson, a character based on Jack A. Johnson, the first African-American heavyweight boxing champion. Johnson had defeated defending champion Tommy Burns in Sydney, Australia, in 1908. *Lucy Kroll Collection, Manuscript Division, Library of Congress.*

The Great White Hope had its world premiere at Arena Stage in Washington on December 12, 1967, with Edwin Sherin as director and Jane Alexander as costar. Sherin sent the script to James Earl Jones, who was in France at the time. Jones immediately wanted to do it. *Lucy Kroll Collection, Manuscript Division, Library of Congress.*

Roger Stevens in his office at the Kennedy Center. Behind him is the Playbill collage given him by his wife Christine showing a great many stage events with which Stevens was associated. *Roger L. Stevens Collection, Music Division, Library of Congress.*

opinion on the merits of their works. John Wharton, a lawyer-member of the group, said of Stevens, "Everyone in the theater took an instant liking to him."

For a while the Stevenses shuttled between New York and Michigan, having friends in both places. Sailing for Europe one summer with the Whartons, Stevens called them to the deck and pointed at the Empire State Building as the ship left New York harbor. "I own that," he seemed to say, as though bemused that the man who owned a six-room house in Ann Arbor also owned the tallest building in the world.

While he worked on at least 40 shows with the Playwrights, he jumped into 30 other Broadway productions, running from the works of T. S. Eliot, Eugene O'Neill, Tennessee Williams and Dylan Thomas to Shakespeare and Shaw, and swung back to Leonard Bernstein with *West Side Story.* He was involved in commercial centers in Seattle and Boston, bought and sold hotels as casually as he might shuffle a poker deck, joined the Volunteers for Adlai Stevenson, and ended up as Chairman of the Democratic Finance Committee for the 1956 campaign—a show that flopped.

When the Playwrights began to decline, Stevens was accused of being remote and sometimes rude. He skimped on their profits, his colleagues said, in order to refund as fully as possible the investors he had persuaded to help stake their shows. Stevens firmly believes in honesty for its own sake. Yet, with his personal blend of pragmatism and idealism, he also never forgets that his future success, his bank credit and his fiscal flexibility, all depend on his honor. He once boasted that "nobody ever loses on my deals," six brave words that he would like to see inscribed on his coat of arms.

Stevens' detractors complain that, for a prominent power in American theater, he is too orthodox, too stuffy in his choice of plays. Possibly so. But at the Kennedy Center with its widely diverse audiences he must provide a balanced selection for many tastes, high and low and in-between brows. What he does provide consistently are high-quality productions with good directors and a generous sprinkling of stars, such as Rex Harrison, Ingrid Bergman, Carol Burnett, Julie Harris, Mickey Rooney, Jill Clayburgh, Douglas Fairbanks, Jr., Jason Robards and Henry Fonda. He accepts the fact that many visitors to Washing-

Agnes de Mille was a Kennedy Center honoree in 1980. De Mille choreographed for two musicals produced in association with Stevens: *Goldilocks,* which opened at New York's Lunt-Fontanne Theatre on October 11, 1958, and *Juno,* 1959. She also served with Stevens on the National Council on the Arts. *Roger L. Stevens Collection, Music Division, Library of Congress.*

ton are thrilled by seeing famous performers in person, so sensibly he makes the most of it.

In his own way, Stevens represents a healthy tendency in America's best noncommercial theaters to operate freely according to the enthusiasms of their directors and the needs of their communities. Across the country, from the Mark Taper Forum in Los Angeles to the Long Wharf Theatre in New Haven, the trend is away from the set patterns of many British acting companies (excellent as they are) toward a more American-style flexibility.

Over the long run Stevens' selection of plays has in fact been surprisingly eclectic. He encouraged and helped back the Phoenix Theatre's wildly untamed *Oh Dad, Poor Dad, Mama's Hung You in the Closet and I'm Feeling So Bad,* and sponsored two more plays by its gifted offbeat author, Arthur Kopit. He backed plays by such innovators as Max Frisch, Federico García Lorca and Jean Genêt. And in effect he subsidized Harold Pinter early in his career by giving him a $1,000 grant to write a new play. In return, Pinter gave Stevens first refusal rights. Stevens has done the same sort of thing for other struggling authors, but, he says, "Pinter was most appreciative."

Stevens is downright captivated by the unorthodox British writer Tom Stoppard, five of whose plays he has backed. Last September, in the Center's Concert Hall, he produced Stoppard's fantastic *Every Good Boy Deserves Favour.* Requiring the entire Pittsburgh Symphony Orchestra, conducted by Andre Previn, as part of the plot, it was too costly a venture for Broadway, but Stevens managed it in Washington with negligible loss, and made its opening night a gala occasion that added luster and prestige to the Center itself.

Stevens began to take root in Washington in 1964 when he was named Chairman of the National Council of the Arts under President Johnson. With an authorized $10 million a year, Stevens set out to stimulate American arts with grants, big and small (he also gave, from his own funds, a substantial sum to Washington's first-rate resident theater, Arena Stage). During the same period he was appointed chairman of the proposed cultural center in the capital, a job so engulfing that he gave up the Council.

The idea for the center, born during the Eisenhower years, kept changing form like a cloud bank in a high wind. Where should it stand? On the Potomac? On the Mall? How much should it cost? $15 million? $75 million? A group of separate buildings? Or all under one roof?

When John F. Kennedy took office, he put Stevens in charge of all the dilemmas and, of course, of raising money. After Kennedy's death, the Center's name was changed to the John F. Kennedy Center for the Performing Arts, and it was also designated as a memorial to the slain President. Then the cash came quicker.

And likewise the opposition. Critics warned that the Potomac site—Stevens' choice—would make the Center inaccessible to the public. The Watergate owners protested that it would jam traffic and keep people from entering their buildings (as if anything could). Many

Facing page:
For many years, Stevens was a member of the executive board of the American Shakespeare Festival Theatre in Stratford, Connecticut, which opened in 1955. World Telegram and Sun *Collection, Prints and Photographs Division, Library of Congress.*

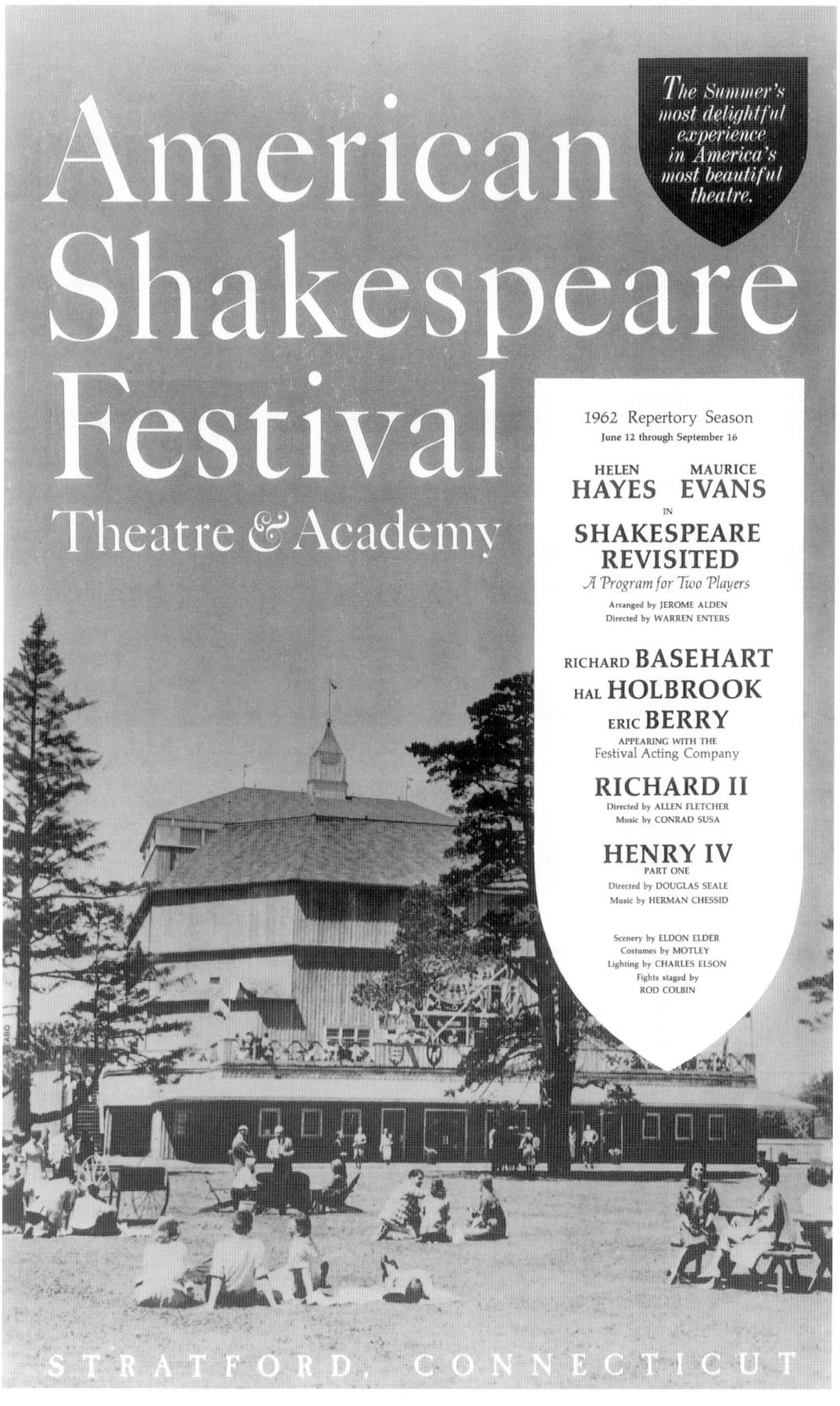

Roger Stevens brought Harold Pinter's *Old Times* to New York in 1971, together with the Royal Shakespeare Festival. Peter Hall directed. The play opened at the Billy Rose Theatre on November 16. Color poster. *Roger Stevens Collection, Music Division, Library of Congress.*

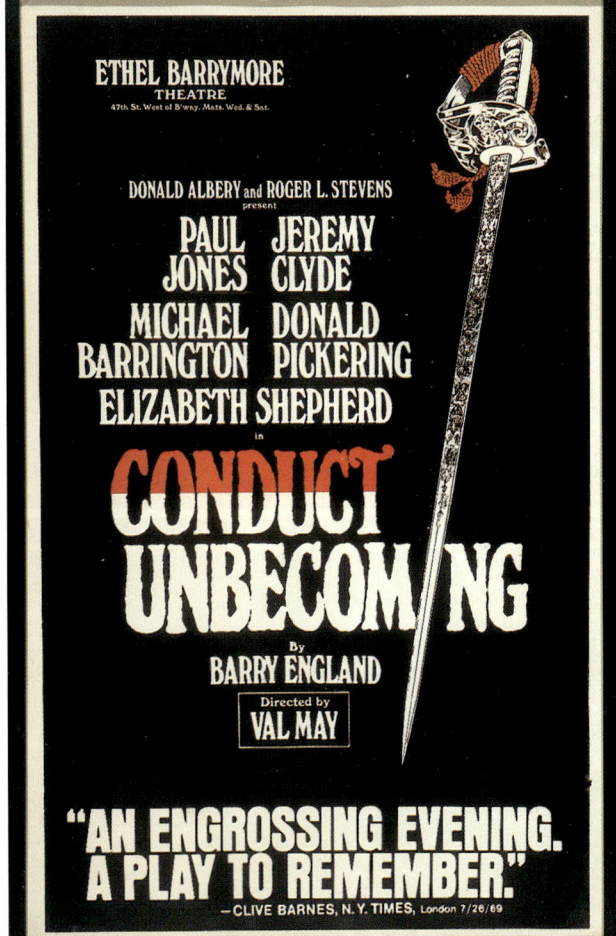

Barry England's play *Conduct Unbecoming* had been a success in its London run at the Queen's Theatre in 1969, produced by Donald Albery, a British producer with whom Stevens was in frequent contact. A comedy set in the late nineteenth century in India in the period of British dominion, it is one of the many plays of merit that Roger Stevens fostered for American production. It opened at New York's Ethel Barrymore Theatre on October 12, 1970. Color poster. *Roger L. Stevens Collection, Music Division, Library of Congress.*

experts scorned Edward Durrell Stone's almost ingenuous design for the Center ("a marble Kleenex box"), hoping for a more grandiose presence, it seemed, and never imagining that in due time Stone's building, with its 66 bronze "tentpoles" holding up the overhanging roof, could take on the festive air of a riverside pavilion.

But Stevens had his own way, and busied himself with both major problems and minutiae. He figured that Stone's plan for trucks to deliver scenery at underground entrances was too costly. The entrances were shifted to street level. He ordered that when shows

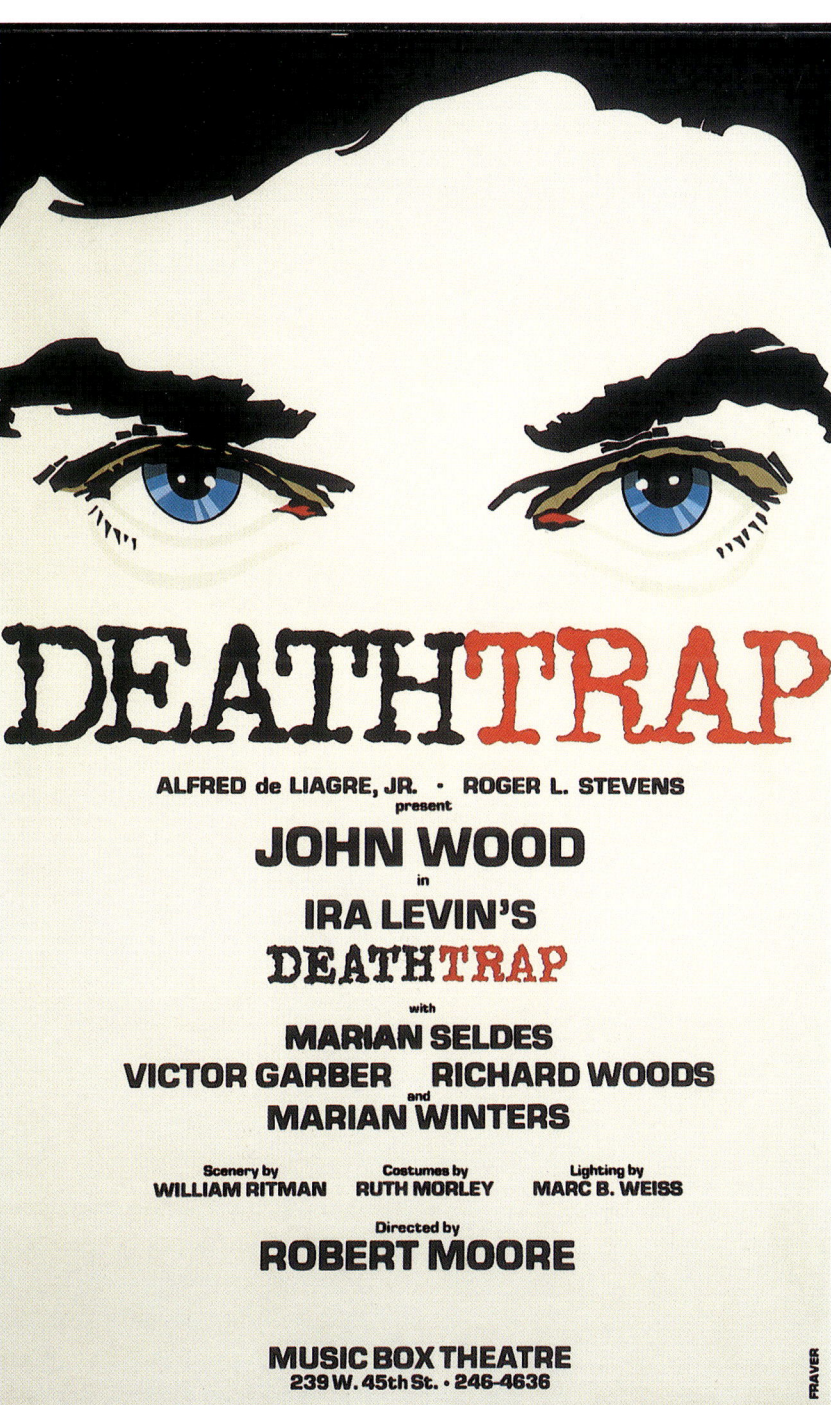

Deathtrap was the only murder mystery with which Stevens was associated and, as was so often the case with productions he presented, it was praised for the high quality of writing and staging as well as for its suspense. It was enormously successful. Color poster. *Roger L. Stevens Collection, Music Division, Library of Congress.*

Pres. John F. Kennedy in Newport, Rhode Island, being shown a model for the National Cultural Center by its architect, Edward Durrell Stone. Roger Stevens is at the left. *Roger L. Stevens Collection, Music Division, Library of Congress.*

were going on at once in the three halls, their curtain times should be staggered to avoid congestion (and, incidentally, to keep the waves of thirsty spectators from overwhelming the bars during intermission).

Stevens' joy in his work hangs largely on one fact: he takes no pay for any of his Center jobs. Being independently rich, he can afford to liberate himself, so to speak, from the profit motive. He can carry on like an impassioned lobbyist, squandering his time, knocking himself out and getting his kicks from running a devilishly intricate and glamorous operation.

Stevens and Feinstein decide on all attractions that come to the Center, though each defers to the other in his field of expertise. Stevens, to be sure, is the theater man, and within the Center the Eisenhower Theater is generally his domain. About a third of all theater productions come from entirely outside sources, and are simply booked into the Eisenhower as they might be into any commercial playhouse, paying the usual fees and percentages to the Center. This season such hits as *Dracula* and *Gin Game* hailed from Broadway, and continued on tour after Washington.

Roger Stevens at the groundbreaking ceremonies for the Kennedy Center on December 2, 1964. Stevens worked tirelessly to raise the funds necessary for the Center, while working simultaneously as chairperson for the National Endowment for the Arts. *Roger L. Stevens Collection, Music Division, Library of Congress.*

But the much larger portion of shows is put together, or helped, by Stevens himself. In the case of *Annie,* one of the biggest musical hits in recent years, the show was aimed at Broadway but ran into trouble during rehearsals when some promised money was withheld. Stevens heard its cry for help, talked to *Annie*'s gifted producer, Mike Nichols, and then, like Daddy Warbucks in the show, helped provide money to rescue Little Orphan Annie. As a result, the Center became one of *Annie*'s coproducers, and has been raking in profits ever since, many of which are plowed into the Center's free educational programs. Stevens makes no money personally on any of these Center operations.

But where does this rescue money come from?

The money comes from a nonprofit subsidiary, a pool of some $500,000. Its funds are guaranteed by a group of public-spirited citizens, who want "to keep the theatrical ball in the air," and who can only lose—not make—money, since any profits go back to the Center. The fund is continually being reduced, and then replenished by box-office profits. So far, the balance of profits and losses has been so well maintained that in six years the original guarantors have never been tapped for additional cash.

Stevens' character is not easy to pin down. Twice it has been said "he has ice in his veins." But in one case it was meant as a compliment to his steady nerves in a crisis, and in the other as a slam on his ruthless drive. Even his admirers praise him in different terms. Deborah Kerr, who starred for him 25 years ago in *Tea and Sympathy,* and is with him now in *The Last of Mrs. Cheyney*, approved him by implication: "I'd rather play Washington than anyplace else." To Tammy Grimes, another Stevens regular, "He is a genius, and a grown-up Tom Sawyer or Huck Finn." To the English star Wendy Hiller, "He is like an American out of a Henry James novel—a large man with a large soul, and I love him." Jason Robards sticks to facts: "Roger gives good parties for his friends. We watch football games together."

His business associates see a moodier, tougher side of Stevens. To Arthur Cantor, a prominent producer, "He's a decent man whose word is his bond. But he's an intensely private person, with a moat around himself. Not the kind of man you'd expect to hug you, but he's hugged the theater all his life. His enthusiasm is his strongest asset."

Victor Samrock, who worked with Stevens during the run of Jean Kerr's *Mary, Mary*, recalls: "He'd stop at the office every month to find out his share of the profits, not to stash away—he had no acquisitive sense—but to invest in something else *interesting*. To him it seemed a crime for money to lie idle. He was fiercely competitive, and not always gracious. He'd yell over the phone, or throw something across the room. But all at once he was gracious again. Never held grudges. No petty malevolence."

Stevens' longest partnership—25 years–is with Robert Whitehead. Their firm, housed in New York's Paramount Building, is entirely apart from Kennedy Center, though once in a while the two operations overlap. Several years ago they both fell in love with *Texas Trilogy*, a series of three plays by a salty new playwright, Preston Jones. It made money for the Center during a 16-week run, but lost on Broadway.

But win or lose, Whitehead enjoys his partner's poker-game nerve: "He's like an old-time American, a frontier gambler."

Old-time American charm runs all through Stevens' rambling house in Georgetown, two miles from the Center. A farmhouse 150 years old, it originally occupied 25 acres, most of which Stevens sold off for town houses. But its rolling lawns, boxwood hedges and rose bushes are still an ideal setting for a large garden party. The house has

Roger Stevens with Sen. Edward Kennedy near the site of the Kennedy Center. Senator Kennedy and many other members of his family have been consistent supporters of the Center's programs. *Roger L. Stevens Collection, Music Division, Library of Congress.*

a long veranda that belongs in the great tradition of American back porches, a shaded hideout with wicker chairs for afternoon reading, iced drinks, dozing off and—for Christine—bird watching. She also welcomes an occasional possum or raccoon, for, as founder and president of the Animal Welfare Institute, she wants animals to feel at home. On her back porch she recently fed pound cake to a possum.

Because Stevens won't wear a wristwatch, Christine gave him a gold watch and chain 15 years ago. He lost it in a phone booth, and swore never again to carry a watch, which for a man who rushes almost daily to airports or conferences seems foolhardy. Yet he has developed an intuitive time sense, and he is backed up by two demon secretaries, in

Washington and New York, who talk to each other by phone and keep their boss "in view" as if he were a fighter plane on a radar screen.

He usually takes vacations by traveling with his wife when she goes to animal welfare conferences. On such outings he tries to get a rest from seeing shows, but rarely succeeds. With her in Australia, he saw a play he liked, brought it both to the Center and Broadway, and now wants to import a whole Australian dramatic festival.

Four years ago the Kennedy Center took over management of the National Theatre in Washington, the city's only big commercial playhouse for shows on tour. It had recently been slumping. Stevens saw it, he says, "as another outlet for theater," which in itself made it irresistible to him. But for his critics it is deplorable: it gives Stevens the power of determining what commercial shows play in Washington. Recently, Stevens got mad at a difficult English star and refused to book her show into the National. He soon changed his mind. But meanwhile the show had to skip Washington and go elsewhere. Ironically, since Stevens has made the capital city more theater-minded, his power makes other producers more alarmed—and more envious.

Kennedy Center is closer to being self-supporting than any other performing arts complex in the world. And, since it is also a memorial to a slain President, it rightly derives funds from the National Park Service. Yet its financial problems are huge. Stevens is now battling Congress for extra time to repay federal loans, and to meet bolt-from-the-blue expenses: repairs on a vast leaky roof; and extra funds to operate a new experimental theater, generously endowed by the Japanese. Every spring the Center transports some 200 college students from across the nation to show their own theater productions in a two-week festival. And so it goes, with a year-round flow of 700 film shows, black theater, concerts, children's entertainment, all crying for lucre in the litany of inflation.

What the Center is doing for the rest of the country

What Roger Stevens and Martin Feinstein are doing for Washington is impressive. But more important is what the example of Kennedy Center is doing for the rest of the country. It enables hundreds of elected government officials, visiting or living in Washington with their families, to observe how a vigorous arts center can benefit a community. Seeing grand productions from La Scala or the Paris Opéra, or the best dramatic actors from the United States and Britain, they get a clearer idea of what the performing arts are all about, and will be better equipped to support them in their own constituencies.

Through it all, Stevens preserves his human dimension. He tends to details, giving $200 to help a favorite bookstore; fussing about moving Henry Fonda and his wife into the Stevens' apartment at the Carlyle Hotel while Fonda was rehearsing in New York for a new Center production, *First Monday in October.* In Christine's absence, he forgets that he is wearing the price tag on a new shirt at a dinner party.

The framework for the Kennedy Center rising on its site on the Potomac. Stevens felt strongly that the proximity of a major freeway artery to the riverside site would be a major asset to the Center. He was proven to be correct. *Roger L. Stevens Collection, Music Division, Library of Congress.*

At times Roger Stevens gives the impression that he is a man trying to be an institution, at other times an institution trying to be a man. It is precisely his efforts in both directions that make him a national asset.

Roger Stevens
An Appreciation

David Richards

I always thought he was the world's oldest boy, but mine was probably not the prevailing opinion. Most people found Roger L. Stevens forbidding. He had, after all, bought and sold the Empire State Building, served as finance chairman of the Democratic Party, produced some 250 Broadway plays, and helped establish the National Council on the Arts, the precursor of today's National Endowments for the Arts and the Humanities. Credentials like those can intimidate.

He was also the man who, defying the odds, escalating costs and a legion of naysayers, built the Kennedy Center for the Performing Arts, which he then ran successfully for seventeen years.

And if that wasn't enough (which it was), his manner discouraged fraternization. He came across as dour. Even people who had known and worked with him for decades referred to him deferentially as Mister Stevens.

He himself acknowledged the problem and chalked it up to what he called his "first-rate negative personality," admitting that "from time to time I've been perceived as a cold fish. The truth is the reason I appear aloof is I'm shy. I inherited it with a lot of other negative qualities I have. Shyness is a stinking trait, I can tell you that. But I just don't like to push in anywhere. I've never done anything I wasn't asked to do. I've been invited to join every club I belong to."

Although he hobnobbed with artists, millionaires, politicians and potentates (and drank with a fair number of them), Stevens opened himself up to relatively few. The social graces were never his. His style of dress was best described as rumpled and he was a poor public speaker. Words, in fact, tended to trip him up, which may be one reason he had such admiration for playwrights and novelists, who used them well.

So why did I persist in the more than twenty-five years I knew him in viewing him as an overgrown boy? It was, first of all, his eyes. They were astonishingly blue and ingenuously clear. I have never seen eyes so expressive. They said everything that Roger Stevens couldn't put into words—that he was forever excited by life and the theater, that his heart sometimes ached, that he liked people far more than he could ever allow himself to let on publicly. Even when he was old and paralyzed, the eyes remained amazingly limpid. Those who thought that Roger Stevens was unapproachable, I suspect, just never looked very deeply into those eyes.

Copyright © David Richards, 2001.

Roger Stevens with Jacqueline Kennedy Onassis, possibly in Mrs. Onassis's New York apartment. Mrs. Onassis was very much involved with Stevens in fund-raising efforts to build the Kennedy Center. *Roger L. Stevens Collection, Music Division, Library of Congress.*

Unmistakably, they were the eyes of an optimist. Even when he was in his seventies, his optimism was that of one who is starting out on life's great adventure and can't wait for the twists and turns ahead. Yet he was no Candide. From first-hand experience, he knew businessmen could be duplicitous, politicians devious, and artists suffocatingly self-centered. But he never strayed from his conviction that "things can always be worked out." Sometimes he felt obliged to add, "One way or another."

There was little bitterness in him, although he could grouse about a bad review and complain about a bad wine. When people let him down, he shrugged and chalked it up to human nature. His optimism, I have come to think, was simply inbred, maybe an extra gene he got that the rest of us didn't, his great gift from the gods. Over his long, fruitful life, it certainly proved to be a self-fulfilling prophecy.

In a society increasingly fixated by celebrity, Roger Stevens was too withdrawn, too enigmatic, to capture the attention of the public at large. We like our celebrities bright and shiny and unequivocal, and if you wanted to know Stevens you had to be able to read between the lines. If you did, however, you saw him for the American Original he really was.

He was the quintessential self-made man, part Mississippi River boat gambler, part cockeyed visionary. There was something of the Roman

Topping out the John F. Kennedy Center for the Performing Arts in Washington, D.C. Pres. John F. Kennedy appointed Stevens to head the effort to build a national cultural center, which was eventually named in the assassinated president's honor. *Roger L. Stevens Collection, Music Division, Library of Congress.*

stoic in him and even a bit of the Lone Ranger, intervening at the last moment to bail out a Broadway show (or a friend) in need.

But until he died in 1996 at the age of eighty-seven, he remained for me The Boy Wonder. The bland ties and the wrinkled suits were a disguise. He looked old, but he thought young. He laughed a lot, even if it was mostly on the inside. As for success, he savored it as much as the next man. Unlike the next man, though, he savored it quietly. And while I'd like to imagine him jumping up and down with delight, when no one was looking, I'm sure he never did. He just got a twinkle in those blue eyes.

The Kennedy Center is such a fixture on the national scene, that it is sometimes forgotten what a protracted struggle it was to get the place built. The legislation mandating its existence was signed by President Eisenhower in 1958, when the idea of a national cultural center was deemed important primarily so that the United States could keep pace culturally with its Cold War nemesis, the Soviet Union.

Nothing much happened, though. Culture has long been vaguely suspect in this country, which tends to view it as the elitist's preserve.

Roger Stevens with Jacqueline Kennedy Onassis and Leonard Bernstein going into the Kennedy Center's Opera House for a performance of Bernstein's *Mass* in June 1972. *Mass* had inaugurated the Opera House and the Kennedy Center in September 1971. *Roger L. Stevens Collection, Music Division, Library of Congress.*

Jacqueline Kennedy Onassis, Joseph Zerbe, Mr. and Mrs. Roger Stevens, Vice-President and Mrs. Nelson Rockefeller, and Mr. and Mrs. Henry Kissinger at the Kennedy Center. *Roger L. Stevens Collection, Music Division, Library of Congress.*

Back then, the government and the arts weren't even strange bedfellows. They dwelled in different houses at opposite ends of the town.

Everything about the proposed center, in fact, would prove to be controversial. The cost, estimated at $15 million (to be raised privately), was judged prohibitive, although by the time the building was completed, the price tag would exceed $77 million. The proposed location on the banks of the Potomac in Foggy Bottom was deemed inaccessible, putting the place out of reach of the common people. And speaking of those people, their tastes would be addressed when it came to programming the auditoriums, wouldn't they?

Pres. John F. Kennedy, sensing that Roger Stevens might be the one man who could forge a national consensus and raise the necessary funds, appointed him chairman of the proposed center in September 1961. It was an inspired choice. Stevens understood the intricacies of big business, moved discreetly in political circles and commanded the respect of the Broadway theatre community. His unique resume made him acceptable to the three constituencies (business, government and arts) that had to come together, if the center was ever to become a reality.

It was painfully slow going at first. Then came Dallas, 1963. In the outpouring of grief that followed the assassination of President Kennedy, it was felt that the Center, with its emphasis on live performances, would be a fitting memorial to the slain president. Congress took to the idea and voted to contribute matching funds. The price tag by this time was hovering around $30 million. But it was still slow going.

At no time in his long career did Stevens come up against so much carping, so many legal and legislative roadblocks, so much red tape as he did in the ensuing years. Pres. Lyndon Johnson broke ground for the center on December 2, 1964, but it was an empty formality. The contractors wouldn't be engaged for another seventeen months.

At one point, when everything looked hopelessly deadlocked, Stevens threw up his hands and said, "Let's just dig a hole in the ground and as soon as it's done, it will stop this acrimony and opposition." In other words, get on with it. It was his lifelong credo.

The Kennedy Center wouldn't open until September 7, 1971, with an emotionally charged production of Leonard Bernstein's *Mass*, which had been specially commissioned for the Opera House. The following night, the National Symphony baptized the Concert Hall. The Eisenhower Theatre wouldn't be ready for another six weeks, while it would take an additional seven years to complete the Terrace Theatre.

"It never occurred to me it wouldn't get done," observed Stevens, phlegmatically. "I've always closed every deal I ever went into."

That the man had reconciled so many opposing forces gave birth to the quip that he could "forge an alliance among a snake, a mongoose, and Eve." Privately, however, Stevens would acknowledge that building the Center was a Sisyphean labor that had required him to raise increasingly greater sums of money, court an ever-changing cast of

Caricature of Eva Le Gallienne by Covarrubias. Le Gallienne was one of the many brilliant actresses seen on the stage of the Kennedy Center's Eisenhower Theatre under Stevens's chairmanship, appearing in 1975 as Fanny Cavendish in *The Royal Family*. *Prints and Photographs Division, Library of Congress.*

Annie opened at New York's Alvin Theatre on April 21, 1977. Roger Stevens recognized the show's potential after its world premiere at the Goodspeed Opera House, and was instrumental in taking it to Broadway. *Broadway Musicals* by Martin Gottfried. *Music Division, Library of Congress.*

Barbara Erwin, Robert Fitch, and Dorothy Loudon give an explosive performance of "Easy Street," Annie's first act curtain number. Before Broadway, the musical played the Eisenhower Theatre in Washington's Kennedy Center. *Broadway Musicals* by Martin Gottfried. *Music Division, Library of Congress.*

As chairman of the Kennedy Center, Stevens worked hard to maintain the highest standards of presentation. The Center's usual drama theatre, the Eisenhower, saw many quality revivals of American plays, including Lillian Hellman's *The Little Foxes*, opening March 1981, with Elizabeth Taylor. *Time*, March 30, 1981. *General Collections, Library of Congress.*

characters in Congress, and continually explain what was for him the institution's obvious raison d'être. He wasn't surprised that he had pulled it off, but he was sometimes amazed by the sheer amount of energy it had consumed.

Paralysis and indecision were his enemies, and too much introspection struck him as suspect. He believed in movement. He didn't shuttle back and forth between Washington and New York so much as he ricocheted between them, sometimes with side trips to Philadelphia or Boston thrown in for good measure. Portable phones being decades away, Stevens thought nothing of conducting high-level negotiations over a pay phone on a busy street corner. Needless to say, he traveled without an entourage. He could move faster that way.

His hectic schedule was inscribed on a plain sheet of paper, ruled off into the hours of the day and the days of the week. His secretary entered his appointments in the appropriate boxes and Stevens carried the paper in the inside left-hand pocket of his suit jacket. Periodically, he would consult it to see when he was expected at a business meeting, a hearing on Capitol Hill or a read-through of a new play. By the week's end, the paper was inevitably worn and tattered.

I was present once, as he was leaving his office late one afternoon. "Let's see," he said, consulting the piece of paper, "I've got dinner at the White House tonight." Then with a perfectly straight face, he added, "What else do I have on?"

One of his associates at the Kennedy Center, the late Richmond Crinkley, recalled coming out of Sardi's Restaurant in New York with Stevens after a luncheon, just as a fire truck was barreling down West 44th Street, sirens wailing. "Roger stopped dead in his tracks and watched it weave in and out of traffic," Crinkley noted. "Then he turned to me and said with complete admiration in his voice, 'Will you look at that sonavagun go!'"

For Crinkley, it was primal evidence that "activity and motion" were fundamental to the man's character. "The most fruitful times I spent with him," he said, "were not when he was in his office or in a theatre, but when he was in a taxi or an airplane or walking down the street, going somewhere. Getting from A to B is what Roger is really all about."

For health reasons, a morning constitutional became an obligatory part of Stevens's routine, once he'd reached his sixties. Whatever the weather, he was a fixture on the streets of Georgetown, where he lived in a stately nineteenth-century farmhouse. On cold days he wore a red knit stocking cap, pulled low. When it was warm, he favored garish sports shirts and pants that sometimes stopped just above his ankles. His preestablished itinerary took him by friends and acquaintances, whom he blithely failed to greet.

"A lot of people see me out walking and I guess I have a bad reputation for ignoring them," he admitted. "Even back in the days when I was going to the University of Michigan in Ann Arbor, they used to jump on me for walking by a good-looking girl without paying attention. All I can say is I don't do it on purpose. I'm just thinking. I do a lot of my problem solving during my walks in the morning. I'm like a rat in a maze."

He was born in Detroit, Michigan, on March 12, 1910, the son of a well-heeled real-estate broker. As befitting his background, he was sent to preparatory school (Choate), but barely muddled through, even though he was expected to go on to Harvard University. Tall, blond, not particularly handsome, but good at cards, he seemed to have the makings of a wastrel about him. Then the Depression hit, erasing the family fortune. Harvard was out. After a year at the University of Michigan in Ann Arbor, Stevens's formal education came to a halt.

He would later say, "The Depression was the best thing that ever happened to me." Indeed, those who were not destroyed by the years of scraping and squalor emerged with a fortified sense of resilience and determination. Stevens was one of them. Living by his wits honed the instinct for self-reliance that was slumbering within him.

The Depression also gave a rich lode of stories that he would occasionally recount, when he was in a mellow mood. There was the time he rode the rails to Montana in search of a job harvesting wheat, only to fail miserably at his first task, which was hitching up a team of horses. Or the time he was working on the Ford assembly line, burnishing gears by holding them up to whirring metal brushes during one of the company's notorious speed-ups. Before long, his hands were a bloody pulp. But he persisted, determined as the sole support of his family to hold on to the job, whatever the costs. Two weeks later, he was fired in a general layoff anyway. The experience made him into a lifelong supporter of the working man and had a lot to do with his changing his political affiliation from Republican to Democrat.

He was pumping gas at night in Detroit for $12 a week, when an armed robber held him up and made off with the receipts—$25. Stevens's supervisor, upon learning the news, chewed him out for having so much cash on hand. "I'd just gone through the trauma of having a gun put in my stomach and his first reaction was I had too much money on me," Stevens recollected. "That did not make me any more friendly toward the business world." Indeed, in the future, Stevens would be his own boss. He was already becoming his own man.

The Depression had provided him with an opportunity to indulge his reflective nature and he seized it. College was out of the question, but the public libraries were free. He haunted them, devouring the great books. "The thing I've always most enjoyed is reading," he said. "I'll never forget this English teacher who lived in the same boarding house I did for a while. She gave me Thomas Mann's *The Magic Mountain* to read. Later she asked me how I liked it. I told her I couldn't read any more than 100 pages a day. She said, 'I'd have been ashamed of you if you had read more.' It's true. Sometimes I feel that some of the famous characters are better friends than the friends I theoretically have."

It was in Ann Arbor that he met the woman who would become his wife, Christine Gesell, at the time a student at the University of Michigan, who was looking to get on with a career. He'd gone into real estate by then and he hired her as a secretary, a job for which she was somewhat ill equipped. She furnished his office with eggplant-colored carpets and a roll-top desk that could be closed at the end of the day, conveniently masking the clutter of papers and documents. Six months later, he proposed marriage. She accepted. (Christine Stevens would go on to become a passionate advocate of animal rights, bringing to the cause all the zeal her husband brought to the theatre.) "Christine could write, paint, and play the piano very well," Stevens recalled. "At the University she had straight As and was terribly good-looking. The fact that someone as well versed as she was, was interested in me, well, that's bound to give you a boost. You can't overlook the good luck I've had in marriage." Did he ever tell her as much? "We're not gushers, either of us," he said, with a dismissive wave of the hand.

Seen here are Kennedy Center honorees Lynn Fontanne, Leontyne Price, James Cagney, Agnes de Mille, and Leonard Bernstein. Begun in 1978, the Honors have achieved national recognition as a major awards event. *Roger L. Stevens Collection, Music Division, Library of Congress.*

As the Depression abated, Stevens's business acumen came to the fore and he began to amass a fortune by trading in undervalued apartment houses and hotels. By 1937, he could claim $50,000 in the bank and a yearly income of $25,000. A decade later, he was considered one of the two most successful entrepreneurs in the country. Long before Donald Trump seized upon the phrase, Stevens had perfected the art of the deal. Dealmaking was, in fact, the sole skill he actively prided himself on.

"I'm supposed to be very intuitive about people, which is why I can put so many deals together," he explained. "I know when to push and when not to push, when to listen and when to talk. I've certainly never had any lack of confidence in my ability to make a deal. But that's really the best of it. For the rest, I'm not very smart. Hell, I'm outsmarted all the time."

After Stevens bought the Empire State Building, the *New Yorker* magazine devoted a two-part profile to him and the complex negotiations that had gone into the multimillion-dollar transaction. Journalism wasn't always his friend, but to the end of his life he viewed that particular article as certification of his worth.

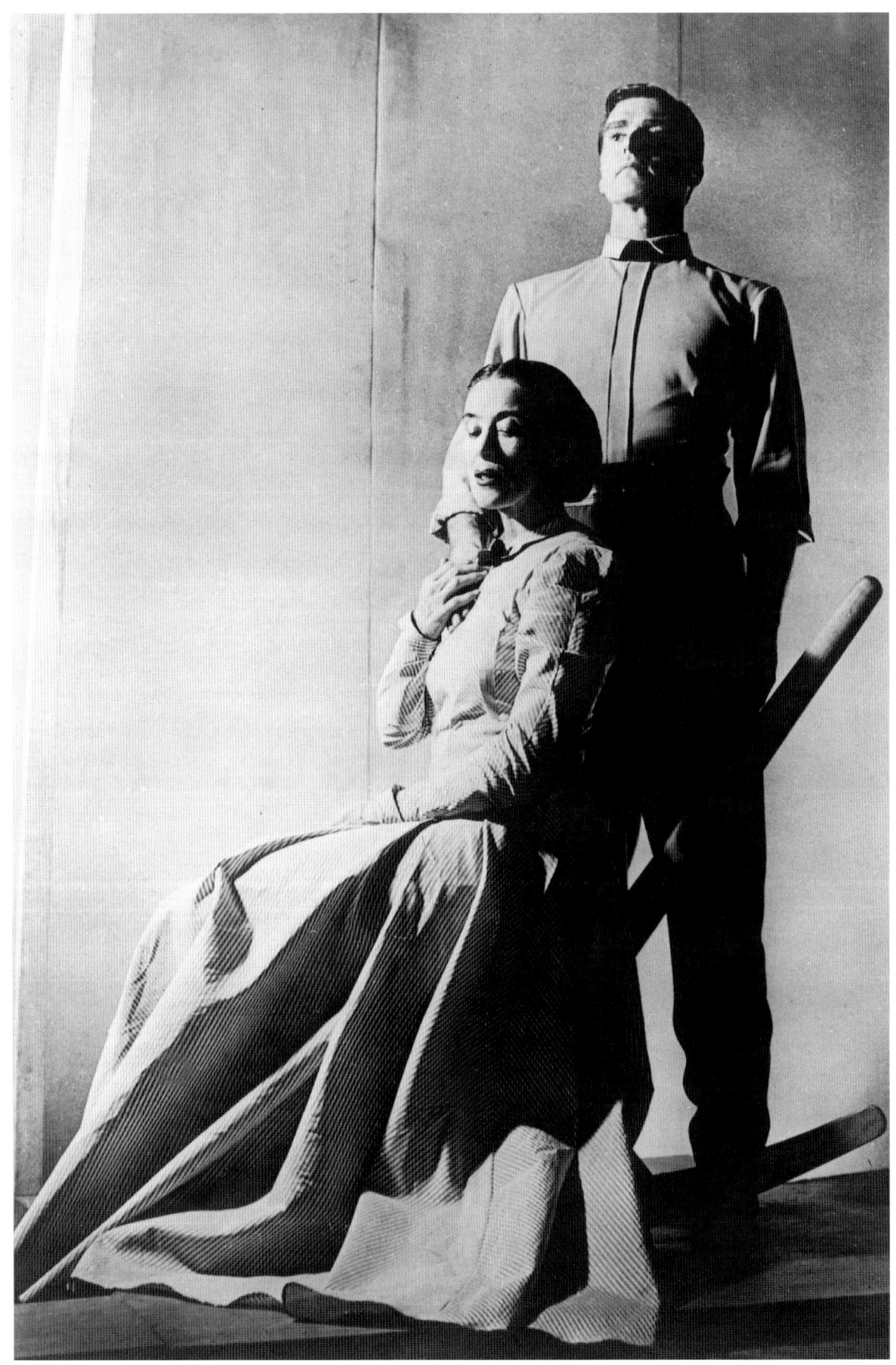

Success as a businessman would not be enough, however. "At the time I purchased the Empire State Building," he explained, "I had as many as 25,000 people working for me. I didn't want to have to worry about their damn lives, about whether this guy's wife was sick with TB or that guy was overdrawn at the bank. So I got out. I always liked to put together a deal for the sake of a deal absurd as that may sound. But the daily operation of business—the buying, the selling, the chiseling—I found it . . . boring!"

Toward the end of the 1940s, this least bohemian of men, inarticulate and physically awkward, was being inexorably drawn to the theatre. It was certainly not for the profits, although Stevens had some galloping hits over the years. Nor was it just for the glamour, although his opening night parties could be star-studded. He liked to say his wife, Christine, had planted the seed, when "she told me that if you didn't go to the theatre, you weren't a civilized person."

But the motivation went deeper. In retrospect, it seems clear that the theatre externalized all that which lay dormant within him ; feelings that he was unable to articulate in other ways, his inner life. If he adored performers, it was to a large degree for their flamboyance, the freedom with which they laid their emotions on the line, their shameless lack of inhibition. He could never do what they did, but he could subsidize their efforts and luxuriate in the performances they gave. In his mind, it was a more than acceptable trade-off.

Stevens's first impulse was to buy himself a theatre in New York City. He took up the idea with Alfred de Liagre, Jr., already a successful producer and soon to become one of Stevens's close friends and associates. De Liagre told him that he was being rash, that it would be more practical to rent a theatre, when he actually had something to produce. In the meantime, shouldn't he acquire some experience by investing in a show or two?

"They never let you in on the good ones," Stevens grumbled.

"Well, I happen to have a good one right here," de Liagre replied.

It was Jean Giraudoux's *The Madwoman of Chaillot*, and the title role, a raffish old lady on a mission to save the world from evil, was to be played by Martita Hunt. Stevens bought into the production, which turned out to be a highlight of the 1948-1949 Broadway season and won Hunt a Tony award for best actress. For his part, Stevens came away with a love of Giraudoux that would last him the rest of his life and an even keener desire to produce shows of his own.

He found one back in Michigan. It was Shakespeare's *Twelfth Night*, which was being performed at the Ann Arbor Drama Festival in 1949 by a cast of professionals. In what now seems a gesture of touching naivete, Stevens moved the production to Broadway. Brooks Atkinson, the respected critic of the *New York Times*, gave it a thumbs up. Audiences stayed away in numbers. And Stevens proceeded to keep the show running until he had lost $45,000 on it.

He had no regrets.

At the time, the regional theatre movement was showing only the

Martha Graham and Erick Hawkins in *Appalachian Spring*, first performed on October 31, 1944, in the Coolidge Auditorium of the Library of Congress. Graham, the most celebrated American choreographer of all time, was one of the Kennedy Center honorees in 1979.
From the Modern Music *Collection. Gift of Minna Lederman, editor of* Modern Music *from 1924 to 1946. Music Division, Library of Congress.*

faintest stirrings of life. Theatre in America meant Broadway, which was enjoying what was arguably its last great flowering before television would change the entertainment habits of the nation forever. Within a few years, Stevens had forged alliances with the American National Theatre and Academy (ANTA) and the esteemed Playwrights' Company, founded by Maxwell Anderson, Elmer Rice, Robert Sherwood, and Sydney Howard to produce their own works on Broadway. ("Sometimes, I'd be sitting in meetings with them, talking about their plays," Stevens recollected, "and I'd say to myself, 'Roger, you haven't even had a college course in literature!'") He had also formed a producing partnership with Robert Whitehead, which would endure until his death.

All at once, he seemed omnipresent.

In 1951, his name as producer could be found on five shows—among then, Ibsen's *Peer Gynt* and Jan de Hartog's *The Fourposter*. In 1953, he had six shows on Broadway, ranging from Jane Bowles's *In the Summer House* to Robert Anderson's hugely successful *Tea and Sympathy*. In 1954, the total was up to eight, a line-up that included T. S. Eliot's *The Confidential Clerk*, Giraudoux's *Ondine* (which would make a star of the young Audrey Hepburn), Maxwell Anderson's *The Bad Seed*, and a musical, *The Golden Apple*, that would remain one of his all-time favorite shows.

The ensuing years brought the likes of *Bus Stop, Tiger at the Gates, Separate Tables, The Waltz of the Toreadors, Orpheus Descending*, the towering *West Side Story, Five Finger Exercise, The Visit* (the final stage appearance of the Lunts), *The Pleasure of His Company, A Touch of the Poet, Duel of Angels* (Giraudoux again!), *The Best Man, Mary, Mary, The Caretaker, A Man for All Seasons, The Milk Train Doesn't Stop Here Anymore, Andorra, The Private Ear* and *The Public Eye, Half a Sixpence, The Homecoming, Indians, A Texas Trilogy*, Edward Albee's Pulitzer Prize-winning *Seascape*, and *First Monday in October*, which paired Henry Fonda and Jane Alexander in a prophetic comedy about the first female Supreme Court justice.

In 1958 alone, he was involved in fifteen Broadway productions. Only his growing commitment to the Center brought those numbers down somewhat in the late 1960s and seventies, although after he retired from the Center, he went right back to Broadway. He had nothing left to prove by then, but as he put it, "I think I'd like to have a few more hits before I roll over and fold up." He got his wish with A. R. Gurney's *The Cocktail Hour* and *Love Letters*.

There were, of course, flops galore. When you produced as much as Stevens did, flops were inevitable. They never seemed to bother him, though. "I never thought there was much point in looking back on events," he said. "I really don't regret anything I've ever done. I just feel that once you've done something—made a fool of yourself or maybe gotten too drunk, which are bad examples—there's no point sitting around crying about it. Theoretically, you should be able to learn a lesson or two along the way, which I don't seem to be able to

Roger Stevens at the Richard L. Coe Awards at the Kennedy Center, sponsored by the new Playwrights' Theatre to honor Audrey Wood. With Coe (left) and Stevens (center) are Todd Bethel, George Grizzard, Morton Gottlieb, Eliott Martin, Richard Barr, and Harry M. Bagdasian. *Roger L. Stevens Collection, Music Division, Library of Congress.*

do too well. But there's not one damn thing you can do about the past."

There was really no other candidate to run the Kennedy Center, once the marble walls were in place and the crystal chandeliers hung. Still, Stevens couldn't breathe easy. To the contrary, it could be argued that getting the building built was the easy part. As a federal memorial, the Center would receive an appropriation from the government only for the maintenance of the public areas. Under no circumstances were government moneys to be used for the actual operation of the theatres. (In the early 1990s, virulent attacks on the National Endowment for the Arts would reveal just how deep the federal mistrust of art and artists still ran.)

No sooner had the Center opened than reams of publicity, fed by the growing mystique surrounding the Kennedy family itself, made it the most visible performing arts center in the nation. In New York City, which prided itself on being the cultural capitol of the nation, skepticism (and jealousy) prevailed. The rest of the country waited to see what would come next, fully expecting something significant. The place could not be allowed to fail.

When it came to opera, music, and dance—essential components of the Center—Stevens was a self-confessed layman. So he created the post of executive director of performing arts (filled initially by Martin Feinstein, later by Marta Istomin) to handle that aspect of the Center's

109

programs. "Roger knew this was an important part of the Center and he enjoyed certain artists, but I'm not sure he enjoyed them musically, if you know what I mean," Feinstein said. "He liked Isaac Stern a lot, but I can't say I saw him at too many Isaac Stern concerts. But as long as I could assure Roger the deficit wouldn't go above a certain amount, there were never any problems."

The theater was Stevens's bailiwick and he eventually had three halls at his disposition: the Eisenhower for plays, the Opera House for musicals, and the Terrace for smaller, quirkier works. Overnight, the Center became the most desirable tryout house in the nation, but that was hardly enough. By the 1970s, Broadway was sending fewer and fewer shows out of town and had yet to discover salvation with such megamusicals as *Cats, Les Miserables* and *The Phantom of the Opera.* To survive, the Center would have to generate much of its own fare.

Stevens promptly set up Kennedy Center Productions, Inc., a non-profit investing arm of the Center, which would finance plays and bank the profits, if there were any. (Recognizing the musical *Annie* as a potential bonanza, KCPI pumped $125,000 into it, then reaped the benefits for years.) More often, though, Stevens was forever raising money to make up the unavoidable deficits. The deadlines were relentless and critics all too ready to pounce when the theatres stayed dark for too long.

If he had a predilection for star-driven vehicles (Ingrid Bergman in *Captain Brassbound's Conversion,* say, or Deborah Kerr in *The Last of Mrs. Cheney*), it was because stars were good for the box office. He produced more than his share of revivals, sometimes out of sheer loyalty to playwrights who had once done well by him. But he saved his greatest enthusiasm for new plays and read every manuscript sent him by agents or budding playwrights, hoping to discover, if not a masterpiece, at least a situation and ideas that absorbed him.

"Finding a worthwhile new play, now that's a thrill that will never get old for me," he said in his trademark mumble, a flat, detached tone that most people use when talking about the weather. To that end, just before leaving the Center, he set up the Kennedy Center Fund for New American Plays, which every year gives enhancement money to a handful of theatres across the country to help them produce works by promising new playwrights. It was a way of priming the pump. "One of my better ideas, if I do say so myself," Stevens allowed himself to boast.

But the ultimate dream was to give the Kennedy Center a resident theatre company of its own. Until he stepped down as chairman in 1987, Stevens never gave up on the idea. Every few years, he would cobble together an embryonic version of what he hoped would evolve into the equivalent of the National Theatre of Great Britain or the Comedie Française.

He made a bold stab in the 1975-1976 season with the American Bicentennial Theatre, a series of ten American plays, which employed overlapping artists and designers. The productions (*Sweet Bird of*

Lara Teeter and Natalia Makarova, as caricatured by Hirschfeld, in "Slaughter on Tenth Avenue," from the revival of Richard Rodgers and Lorenz Hart's *On Your Toes*. Stevens was one of the presenters of this revival seen at the Kennedy Center's Opera House before opening in New York on March 6, 1983. *Roger Stevens Collection, Music Division, Library of Congress.*

Youth, The Royal Family, The Heiress) were meritorious, but when the Bicentennial hoop-la was over, so, alas, was that particular company. Eight years later, he resuscitated the charter of the American National Theatre and Academy, with which he had worked in his early days as a New York producer, and moved the dormant organization to the Center.

At the head of the American National Theatre, as it was called, he appointed an iconoclastic young director, Peter Sellars, whose radically conceived productions included *The Count of Monte Cristo*, Chekhov's *Seagull* with laser beams, and the Greek tragedy *Ajax*, featuring in the title role a hearing-impaired actor, who delivered his part in sign language. Audiences were generally flummoxed (so was Stevens on occasion), and the enterprise lasted barely two years.

To this day, however, it remains the Center's most daring theatrical undertaking. Stevens, then in his seventy-fourth year, had never invested so much of himself in a young director and a resident troupe. Regrettably, Stevens's successors would quickly abandon the ideal of theatrical self-sufficiency, and the Center would take a much less active role in determining its own fare. For now, at any rate, a significant part of Stevens's vision has been lost.

As a producer, he may have lacked the outrageous promotional skills of a David Merrick, Broadway's Abominable Showman. And he never nurtured the close, paternalistic ties that Joseph Papp forged with the playwrights who called the Public Theatre in New York their home. He was not a "hands-on" man. He hired others and then stepped aside, trusting them to give their best effort, which meant that most theatre people loved to work for him.

Although the producing ego is usually a large one, Stevens kept his in check, so fellow producers were no less eager to team up with him. And they did—everyone from Binkie Beaumont, Frederick Brisson, Lyn Austin, Donald Seawell, and Lars Schmidt, to the two New York powerhouses, the Shuberts and the Nederlanders. Even one Claus Von Bulow came briefly on board with *Wings,* a devastating study of a stroke victim.

Looking back, it is incontestable that Stevens's eclecticism, his pragmatism, and his vast network of theatrical contacts were exactly what the Center needed at the time; not to mention his shambling modesty.

The intelligentsia sniffed. But those who dismissed Stevens as a businessman with commercial tastes conveniently forgot that he championed the young Harold Pinter, Tom Stoppard, and Arthur Kopit. That he was there repeatedly for Tennessee Williams, Arthur Miller, and William Inge. And that among his favorite playwrights, he counted Luigi Pirandello, who viewed man as an unfathomable creature of multiple and often contradictory personalities; Friedrich Duerrenmatt, whose parables of corruption and venality are among the theatre's darkest; and, of course, Giraudoux, that most elegant of French dramatists.

Granted, if you expected Stevens to articulate his guiding aesthetic, you were in for a letdown. Nothing irritated him more than to have someone ask him about the "artistic direction" of the Kennedy Center. He had little patience for theoretical hairsplitting. The critical dialogue with its emphasis on themes and character development interested him not a whit.

Pressed on one occasion to define his producing philosophy, he responded, "I am reminded of a conversation between Lennie Bernstein and Alvin Ailey, before *Mass* opened. Lennie is a great intellectual and he was asking Alvin how he choreographed. 'I don't know,' Alvin said. 'I just get those people up there on the stage and I tell them to

Leontyne Price, one of the greatest operatic sopranos of modern times, with Roger and Christine Stevens. Ms. Price was a Kennedy Center honoree in 1980. *Roger L. Stevens Collection, Music Division, Library of Congress.*

move this way and then I tell them to move that way.' And Lennie said, 'Yes, but the theory behind it, you must have a *theory!*' And Alvin said, 'Not really. All I do is get them up there and move them around so they look pretty.'

"Well, it was one of the greatest conversations I ever heard in my life. Really, very, very funny. I certainly wouldn't want to equate myself with either of those men. They're both geniuses. My point is, that's the way I work. I don't have any deep theories. I try to find the best playwrights I can and I try to do different kinds of plays because I think Washington demands a varied diet, and basically . . . well . . . that's it."

And that *was it.*

"Roger really was a mystery in that respect," acknowledged Robert Whitehead, with whom Stevens produced some of his most distinguished Broadway hits. "He never discussed a play with any sense of wonderment about what makes it happen on the stage. The interior

life of a play or the reasons why plays are written are endlessly fascinating to me. I don't think Roger cared to seek that out. He would always palm all the artistic discussion off on me. But maybe that's good. Maybe the rest of us are phonies. Roger just had this basic sense that doing enough of these plays would somehow be good for the world.

"He was a facilitator. He enjoyed the fact that someone would call him up and say, 'We're desperate. We need another $50,000.' For him, the thrill was helping get it together, money-wise. He was utterly fearless, when it came to money. I think he saw it as a river running by, something you bathed in now and then.

"A while ago, the Center was going to celebrate Roger, and Supreme Court Justice Abe Fortas asked me to get involved in planning the tribute. I said, 'Abe, let's not just have someone get up and sing or play the piano. Let's do something connected with Rog.' And Fortas said, 'If you're going to do something personal, then you should bring out a wagon filled with hundred dollar bills and set it on fire!'"

In the worlds of film, painting, and literature, one generation's work can be visited by the next. The theatre, however, is ephemeral. "Here today, gone today" is its motto. It exists only in the present tense, almost as if the falling curtain erases what has just transpired on the stage. So the question naturally arises: What is Stevens's legacy?

He definitely left behind a huge body of plays that might not otherwise have seen the light of day. Some will continue to be performed in the twenty-first century. On the other hand, it would be foolhardy not to recognize that fashions change and nothing goes out of date faster than the play that claims to have its finger on the pulse of the times. (*West Side Story* is very likely to be part of our permanent theatrical repertory. *Under the Yum Yum Tree* is not.)

He left behind a majestic building, an instant landmark as soon as it opened, as much a part of the Washington landscape as the Lincoln Memorial and the Washington Monument. Hordes visit it annually. The Kennedy Center honors, which are bestowed each year upon the country's most popular artists, have served to anchor the institution in the public consciousness as a place of value and excellence. But buildings necessarily take on identities of their own, independent of those who brought them into being. (Quick now, who put up the Empire State Building?) While proposals to name the Terrace Theatre after Stevens have been advanced periodically, none has been acted upon and only a bust of the man in the Hall of States serves as a tangible reminder of his huge contribution to the place.

So I like to believe that he left something else behind, something more ineffable, but something ultimately more crucial than the red-velvet theatres and stately marbled halls. The Center is but an edifice. What animates it is faith—faith that the arts are worthwhile, that a world without them is a poor place, indeed, and that decent and honorable men and women everywhere have a responsibility to keep them alive.

Drawn in 1938, this Covarrubias caricature is rich in Roger Stevens associations which were yet to come: Alfred Lunt and Lynn Fontanne in S. N. Behrman's *Amphitryon 38*, done for the Playwrights' Company, and adapted from Giraudoux; and Kennedy Center honorees Benny Goodman, Ginger Rogers, Fred Astaire, Shirley Temple, and Lynn Fontanne. *Prints and Photographs Division. Library of Congress.*

That was the belief that galvanized Stevens. He could only express it haltingly, but it gave him the will to persevere, when others would have walked away, disheartened. Time and again, it allowed him to transcend himself. In the end, it endowed him with an odd kind of nobility. Anyone who embraces that faith is perpetuating what was the very best of the man.

As he got older, the killing pace took its toll. Starting in his sixties, he had a series of heart attacks. Characteristically, he made little of them and brushed away anyone who tried to fuss over his health. Heart attacks were nuisances. Hospitals were temporary abodes. Each time, he bounced back. He seemed indestructible.

In September 1993, however, he suffered a stroke that paralyzed his right side. Then, while he was undergoing treatment at Georgetown University Hospital, a second stroke robbed him of most of his speech. From that point on, until his death three years later, he was confined to a wheelchair. At meals he had to be helped with his food. To visit him was painful. He would start to say something, but after a few words, articulated with difficulty, the sentence would dry up in his mouth and he would be unable to complete it.

He, who had embodied the principle of perpetual motion, was locked in a terrible prison.

What his friends did was sit with him in the living room of the Georgetown house and chat with him. It was necessarily a one-way conversation. But he liked hearing about what was going on in their lives, the plays they'd seen, the projects they were working on. He would listen and nod and understand, I'm sure.

And all the time, he would be looking at you with those eyes. Those blue, blue eyes. Still filled with wonder, still clear as a summer's sky, they remained young to the absolute end.

Roger Stevens was a presenter of the award-winning revival of *She Loves Me* when it transferred to the Brooks Atkinson Theatre in New York, opening on September 28, 1993. The Roundabout Theatre Company had opened the production on June 10, 1993, at the Criterion Center Stage Rights. Color poster. *Roger L. Stevens Collection, Music Division, Library of Congress.*

Overview of the Roger L. Stevens Collection

The Roger L. Stevens Collection was given to the Library of Congress by Roger and Christine Stevens over a period of time, beginning in 1995. It documents Stevens's careers—in theatrical production, cultural affairs and real estate—and spans a period of more than fifty years. It includes material on Stevens's work as a significant force in the development, construction, and administration of the John F. Kennedy Center for the Performing Arts in Washington, D.C., and his role in the history of the National Endowment for the Arts. It contains documentation on Stevens's activities with many other cultural institutions which Stevens served, often as a member of the board. These include the Metropolitan Opera Company in New York City. The files on his theatre productions include coverage of his work with, among other theatre groups, Playwrights Company, Producers Theatre, and Whitehead-Stevens, as well as the American National Theatre and Academy, the Phoenix Theatre in New York City, and the American Shakespeare Festival in Stratford, Connecticut.

The collection consists of theatrical production files, real estate project files, correspondence files, personal papers, calendars, records of telephone calls, theatrical posters, awards, photographs, playbills, newspaper clippings, contracts, and video tapes.

The primary subdivisions within the collection are theatrical production files, arranged by title of play or musical production; real estate arranged alphabetically by organization name; correspondence to and from organizations, organized alphabetically by organization name; correspondence to and from individuals, arranged alphabetically by correspondent; chronologically arranged correspondence files; general subject files, exclusive of correspondence; correspondence/telephone logs; Stevens's personal papers; Stevens's writings and speeches; playbill files arranged alphabetically by theater title; and photograph files.

The material on play production includes documentation on plays actually produced by Stevens, either directly or through an organization, as well as on plays that Stevens considered producing that were ultimately produced by another producing office, and play projects that never even reached the production stage. Because the theater was so much a critical focus for Stevens, documentation of these projects is found in abundance in several of the subdivisions. These constitute a remarkable research source for American theatre based in New York, particularly in the 1950s and early 1960s, before Stevens's commitment of so much of his time to fostering the success of the Kennedy Center and the NEA.

The photograph files include images of the Kennedy Center under construction and of Mr. and Mrs. Stevens with a number of persons in the arts and in government—including several presidents and their first ladies—as well as coverage of aspects of Stevens's personal life.

The Stevens Collection is available to readers and researchers through the Performing Arts Reading Room of the Library of Congress in the Library's Madison Building.

Roger L. Stevens's Productions 1949-1987

Roger L. Stevens was associated with the theatrical production of a vast number of plays, either as part of a producing organization (such as the Playwrights' Company), in association with another producer, or independently. The following is a list (as complete as possible), in chronological order, of productions undertaken by Mr. Stevens in one or another of these capacities. The opening night date appears at the end of each entry.

1949   *Twelfth Night.* Play by William Shakespeare. Produced by Roger L. Stevens. Empire Theatre, New York, New York. October 3, 1949.

1950   *Peter Pan.* Play by J. M. Barrie, with music by Leonard Bernstein. Presented by Peter Lawrence and Roger L. Stevens. Imperial Theatre, New York, New York. April 24, 1950.

The Cellar and the Well. Play by Philip Pruneau. Presented by George Freedley and Roger L. Stevens. ANTA Playhouse, New York, New York. December 10, 1950.

1951   *Peer Gynt.* Play by Henrik Ibsen. Presented by Cheryl Crawford in association with Roger L. Stevens. ANTA Playhouse, New York, New York. January 28, 1951.

The Fourposter. Play by Jan de Hartog. Presented by the Playwrights' Company. Ethel Barrymore Theatre, New York, New York. October 24, 1951.

Barefoot in Athens. Play by Maxwell Anderson. Presented by the Playwrights' Company. Martin Beck Theatre, New York, New York. October 31, 1951.

The Grand Tour. Play by Elmer Rice. Presented by the Playwrights' Company. Martin Beck Theatre, New York, New York. December 10, 1951.

1952   *Mr. Pickwick.* Play by Stanley Young. Presented by the Playwrights' Company. Plymouth Theatre, New York, New York. September 17, 1952.

1953   *The Emperor's Clothes.* Play by George Tabori. Presented by the Playwrights' Company with Robert Whitehead. Ethel Barrymore Theatre, New York, New York. February 9, 1953.

Sabrina Fair. Play by Samuel Taylor. Presented by the Playwrights' Company. National Theatre, New York, New York. February 9, 1953.

Tea and Sympathy. Play by Robert Anderson. Presented by the Playwrights' Company. Ethel Barrymore Theatre, New York, New York. September 30, 1953.

Escapade. Play by Roger MacDougal. Presented by Alfred de Liagre, Jr. and Roger L. Stevens. 48th Street Theatre, New York, New York. November 18, 1953.

In the Summer House. Play by Jane Bowles. Presented by the Playwrights' Company with Oliver Smith. Playhouse Theatre, New York, New York. December 29, 1953.

The Remarkable Mr. Pennypacker. Play by Liam O'Brien. Presented by Robert Whitehead and Roger L. Stevens. Coronet Theatre, New York, New York. December 30, 1953.

1954 *The Confidential Clerk.* Play by T. S. Eliot. Presented by Henry Sherek and the Producers Theatre. Morosco Theatre, New York, New York. February 11, 1954.

The Winner. Play by Elmer Rice. Presented by the Playwrights' Company. Playhouse Theatre, New York, New York. February 17, 1954.

Ondine. Play by Jean Giraudoux. Presented by the Playwrights' Company. 46th Street Theatre, New York, New York. February 18, 1954.

The Golden Apple. Musical by Jerome Moross and John Latouche. Presented by the Phoenix Theatre and Roger L. Stevens. Phoenix Theatre, New York, New York. March 11, 1954.

All Summer Long. Play by Robert Anderson. Presented by the Playwrights' Company. Coronet Theatre, New York, New York. September 23, 1954.

The Traveling Lady. Play by Horton Foote. Presented by the Playwrights' Company. Playhouse Theatre, New York, New York. October 27, 1954.

The Bad Seed. Play by Maxwell Anderson. Presented by the Playwrights' Company. 46th Street Theatre, New York, New York. December 8, 1954.

The Flowering Peach. Play by Clifford Odets. Presented by the Producers' Theatre. Belasco Theatre, New York, New York. December 28, 1954.

1955 *The Dark Is Light Enough.* Play by Christopher Fry. Presented by Katherine Cornell and Roger L. Stevens. ANTA Theatre, New York, New York. February 23, 1955.

Bus Stop. Play by William Inge. Presented by Robert Whitehead and Roger L. Stevens. Music Box Theatre, New York, New York. March 2, 1955.

Cat on a Hot Tin Roof. Play by Tennessee Williams. Presented by the Playwrights' Company. Morosco Theatre, New York, New York. March 24, 1955.

Once Upon a Tailor. Musical by Mary Rodgers and Baruch Lumet. Presented by the Playwrights' Company with George Boroff. Cort Theatre, New York, New York. May 23, 1955.

Memory of Two Mondays. View from the Bridge. Two plays by Arthur Miller. Presented by Kermit Bloomgarden and Whitehead/Stevens. Coronet Theatre, New York, New York. September 29, 1955.

Tiger at the Gates. Play by Jean Giraudoux. Presented by the Playwrights' Company with Henry Margolis. Plymouth Theatre, New York, New York. October 3, 1955.

Island of Goats. Play by Ugo Betti. Presented by Roger L. Stevens and Hardy Smith, Ltd. Fulton Theatre, New York, New York. October 4, 1955.

1956 *Tamburlaine the Great.* Play by Christopher Marlowe. Presented by Producers' Theatre in association with Stratford, Connecticut. Winter Garden Theatre, New York, New York. January 19, 1956.

The Ponder Heart. Play by Joseph Fields and Jerome Chodorov. Presented by the Playwrights' Company. Music Box Theatre, New York, New York. February 16, 1956.

The Lovers. Play by Leslie Stevens. Presented by Gayle Stein with the Playwrights' Company. Martin Beck Theatre, New York, New York. May l0, 1956.

Separate Tables. Play by Terence Rattigan. Presented by the Producers' Theatre in association with Hecht-Lancaster. Music Box Theatre, New York, New York. October 25, 1956.

Major Barbara. Play by George Bernard Shaw. Presented by Robert Joseph and the Producers' Theatre. Martin Beck Theatre, New York, New York. October 30, 1956.

The Sleeping Prince. Play by Terence Rattigan. Presented by the Producers' Theatre and Gilbert Miller. Coronet Theatre, New York, New York. November 1, 1956.

1957 *A Small War on Murray Hill*. Play by Robert Sherwood. Presented by the Playwrights' Company. Ethel Barrymore Theatre, New York, New York. January 3, 1957.

A Clearing in the Woods. Play by Arthur Laurents. Presented by Roger L. Stevens and Oliver Smith. Belasco Theatre, New York, New York. January l0, 1957.

The Waltz of the Toreadors. Play by Jean Anouilh. Presented by the Producers' Theatre. Coronet Theatre, New York, New York. January 14, 1957.

A Hole in the Head. Play by Arnold Schulman. Presented by the Producers' Theatre. Plymouth Theatre, New York, New York. February 28, 1957.

The Sin of Pat Muldoon. Play by John McLiam. Presented by Richard Adler and Roger L. Stevens. Cort Theatre, New York, New York. March 13, 1957.

Orpheus Descending. Play by Tennessee Williams. Presented by the Producers' Theatre. Martin Beck Theatre, New York, New York. March 21, 1957.

West Side Story. Musical based on a conception by Jerome Robbins. Book by Arthur Laurents. Music by Leonard Bernstein. Lyrics by Stephen Sondheim. Presented by Robert E. Griffiths and Harold S. Prince by arrangement with Roger L. Stevens. Winter Garden Theatre, New York, New York. September 26, 1957.

A Boy Growing Up. Play by Emlyn Williams. Presented by Sol Hurok in association with Roger L. Stevens. Longacre Theatre, New York, New York. October 7, 1957.

Under Milkwood. Play by Dylan Thomas. Presented by Gilbert Miller, Henry Sherek, and Roger L. Stevens. Henry Miller's Theatre, New York, New York. October 15, 1957.

Time Remembered. Play by Jean Anouilh. Presented by the Playwrights' Company in association with Milton Sperling. Morosco Theatre, New York, New York. November 12, 1957.

Nude with Violin. Play by Noel Coward. Presented by the Playwrights' Company, Lance Hamilton, and Charles Russell. Belasco Theatre, New York, New York. November 14, 1957.

The Rope Dancers. Play by Morton Wishengrad. Presented by the Playwrights' Company and Gilbert Miller. Cort Theatre, New York, New York. November 20, 1957.

The Country Wife. Play by William Wycherly. Presented by the Playwrights' Company, Malcolm Wells, and Daniel Blum. Adelphi Theatre, New York, New York. November 27, 1957.

1958 *Summer of the 17th Doll*. Play by Ray Lawler. Presented by the Theatre Guild and the Playwrights' Company, by arrangement with the Elizabethan Theatre Trust and St. James Plaayers, Ltd. Coronet Theatre, New York, New York. January 22, 1958.

Present Laughter. Play by Noel Coward. Presented by the Playwrights' Company, Lance Hamilton, and Charles Russell. Belasco Theatre, New York, New York. January 31, 1958.

Joyce Grenfell Requests the Pleasure. By Joyce Grenfell. Presented by Roger L. Stevens and Laurier Lister. Lyceum Theatre, New York, New York. April 7, 1958.

The Firstborn. Play by Christopher Fry. Presented by Katherine Cornell and Roger L. Stevens. Coronet Theatre, New York, New York. April 29, 1958.

The Visit. Play by Friedrich Duerrenmatt. Presented by the Producers' Theatre. Lunt-Fontanne Theatre, New York, New York. May 5, 1958.

Howie. Play by Phoebe Ephron. Presented by the Playwrights' Company, John M. Slevin, and John Gerstad. 46th Street Theatre, New York, New York. September 17, 1958.

A Handful of Fire. Play by N. Richard Nash. Presented by David Susskind and the Playwrights' Company. Martin Beck Theatre, New York, New York. October 1, 1958.

A Touch of the Poet. Play by Eugene O'Neill. Presented by the Producers' Theatre. Helen Hayes Theatre, New York, New York. October 2, 1958.

Goldilocks. Musical. Book by Walter and Jean Kerr. Music by Leroy Anderson. Presented by the Producers' Theatre. Lunt-Fontanne Theatre, New York, New York. October 11, 1958.

The Pleasure of His Company. Play by Samuel Taylor with Cornelia Otis Skinner. Presented by Frederick Brisson and the Playwrights' Company. Longacre Theatre, New York, New York. October 22, 1958.

The Man in the Dog Suit. Play by Albert Reich and William Wright. Presented by the Producers' Theatre. Coronet Theatre, New York, New York. October 30, 1958.

Edwin Booth. Play by Milton Geiger. Presented by Jose Ferrer and the Playwrights' Company. 46th Street Theatre, New York, New York. November 24, 1958.

Cue for Passion. Play by Elmer Rice. Presented by the Playwrights' Company and Franchot Productions. Henry Miller's Theatre, New York, New York. November 25, 1958.

The Cold Wind and the Warm. Play by S. N. Behrman. Presented by the Producers' Theatre and Robert Whitehead Productions. Morosco Theatre, New York, New York. December 8, 1958.

The Gazebo. Play by Alec Coppel. Presented by the Playwrights' Company and Frederick Brisson. Lyceum Theatre, New York, New York. December 12, 1958.

1959 *Look After Lulu*. Play by Noel Coward. Presented by the Playwrights' Company, Gilbert Miller, Lance Hamilton, and Charles Russell. Henry Miller's Theatre, New York, New York. March 3, 1959.

Juno. Musical. Based on Sean O'Casey's *Juno and the Paycock*. Book by Joseph Stein. Music and lyrics by Marc Blitzstein. Presented by the Playwrights' Company, Oliver Smith, and Oliver Rea. Winter Garden Theatre, New York, New York. March 9, 1959.

Much Ado About Nothing. Play by William Shakespeare. Presented by the Cambridge Drama Festival by arrangement with the Producers' Theatre. Lunt-Fontanne Theatre, New York, New York. September 17, 1959.

Chéri. Play by Anita Loos. Presented by the Playwrights' Company and Robert Lewis. Morosco Theatre, New York, New York. October 12, 1959.

The Flowering Cherry. Play by Robert Bolt. Presented by the Playwrights' Company and Don Herbert. Lyceum Theatre, New York, New York. October 21, 1959.

Five Finger Excercise. Play by Peter Shaffer. Presented by Frederick Brisson and the Playwrights' Company. Music Box Theatre, New York, New York. December 2, 1959.

Silent Night, Lonely Night. Play by Robert Anderson. Presented by the Playwrights' Company. Morosco Theatre, New York, New York. December 3, 1959.

1960 *The Tumbler*. Play by Benn W. Levy. Presented by Alfred de Liagre, Jr. and Roger L. Stevens in association with Laurence Olivier. Helen Hayes Theatre, New York, New York. February 24, 1960.

The Best Man. Play by Gore Vidal. Presented by the Playwrights' Company. Morosco Theatre, New York, New York. March 31, 1960.

Duel of Angels (*Pour Lucrece*). Play by Jean Giraudoux. Presented by Roger L. Stevens and Sol Hurok. Helen Hayes Theatre, New York, New York. April 19, 1960.

Rosemary. Play by Molly Kazan. Presented by Roger L. Stevens. York Playhouse, New York, New York. November 14, 1960.

The Alligators. Play by Molly Kazan. Presented by Roger L. Stevens. York Playhouse, New York, New York. November 14, 1960.

Under the Yum Yum Tree. Play by Lawrence Roman. Presented by Frederick Brisson and Roger L. Stevens. Henry Miller's Theatre, New York, New York. November 16, 1960.

1961 *The Conquering Hero*. Musical. Based on the motion picture, *Hail the Conquering Hero*. Book by Larry Gelbart. Music by Moose Charlap. Lyrics by Noram Gimbel. Presented by Robert Whitehead and Roger L. Stevens. ANTA Theatre, New York, New York. January 16, 1961.

Julia, Jake, and Uncle Joe. Play by Howard M. Teichmann. Presented by Roger L. Stevens and John Shubert in association with S. S. Krellberg. Booth Theatre, New York, New York. January 28, 1961.

Midgie Purvis. Play by Mary Chase. Presented by Robert Whitehead and Roger L. Stevens in association with Alfred R. Glancey, Jr. Martin Beck Theatre, New York, New York. February 1, 1961.

Mary, Mary. Play by Jean Kerr. Presented by Roger L. Stevens. Martin Beck Theatre, New York, New York. March 8, 1961.

The Importance of Being Oscar. A reading of Oscar Wilde's plays, letters, and poems. Arranged and acted by Micheal MacLiammoir. Produced by Sol Hurok and Roger L. Stevens in association with Michael Redgrave and Fred Sadoff. Lyceum Theatre, New York, New York. March 14, 1961.

A Far Country. Play by Henry Denker. Presented by Roger L. Stevens and Joel Schenker. Music Box Theatre, New York, New York. April 4, 1961.

The Caretaker. Play by Harold Pinter. Presented by Roger L. Stevens, Frederich Brisson, and Gilbert Miller. Lyceum Theatre, New York, New York. October 4, 1961.

Blood, Sweat, and Stanley Poole. Play by James and William Goldman. Presented by Roger L. Stevens and Fields Productions. Associate producer, Lyn Austin. Morosco Theatre, New York, New York. October 5, 1961.

Everybody Loves Opal. Play by John Patrick. Presented by Roger L. Stevens in association with Seven Arts Productions. Longacre Theatre, New York, New York. October 11, 1961.

A Man for All Seasons. Play by Robert Bolt. Presented by Robert Whitehead and Roger L. Stevens. ANTA Theatre, New York, New York. November 22, 1961.

First Love. Play by Samuel Taylor. Presented by Roger L. Stevens and Frederick Brisson in association with Samuel Taylor. Morosco Theatre, New York, New York. December 25, 1961.

1962 *Romulus*. Play by Gore Vidal. Presented by Roger L. Stevens in association with Henry Guettel. Music Box Theatre, New York, New York. January 10, 1962.

Oh Dad, Poor Dad, Mamma's Hung You in the Closet and I'm Feelin' So Sad. Play by Arthur Kopit. Staged by Jerome Robbins. Presented by T. Edward Hambleton and Norris Houghton, by arrangement with Roger L. Stevens. Phoenix Theatre, New York, New York. February 26, 1962.

Tender Loving Care. Play by Elena Miramova. Presented by Roger L. Stevens. Cocoanut Playhouse, Miami, Florida. Spring 1962.

The Magnificent Gourmet. Play by Joseph Schrank. Presented by E. P. Clift and Roger Stevens. Lyceum Theatre, Sheffield, England. March 26, 1962.

The Father. Play by August Strindberg. Presented by the Royal Dramatic Theatre of Sweden, under the auspices of the Seattle World's Fair, Performing Arts Division, and Roger L. Stevens. Cort Theatre, New York, New York. May 14, 1962.

Long Day's Journey into Night. Play by Eugene O'Neill. Presented under the auspices of the Seattle World's Fair, Performing Arts Division, and Roger L. Stevens. Cort Theatre, New York, New York. May 15, 1962.

Miss Julie. Play by August Strindberg. Presented under the auspices of the Seattle World's Fair, Performing Arts Division, and Roger L. Stevens. Cort Theatre, New York, New York. May 16, 1962.

Judith. Play by Jean Giraudoux. Presented by Roger L. Stevens. Her Majesty's Theatre, London, UK. June 20, 1962.

Banderol. Play by Dore Schary. Presented by Robert Whitehead and Roger L. Stevens. Playhouse Theatre, New York, New York. September 13, 1962.

Step on a Crack. Play by Bernard Euslin. Presented by Roger L. Stevens and Herbert Swope, Jr. Ethel Barrymore Theatre, New York, New York. October 17, 1962.

Calculated Risk. Play by Joseph Hayes. Presented by Howard Erskine, Roger L. Stevens, and Joseph Hayes. Ambassador Theatre, New York, New York. October 31, 1962.

Tiger, Tiger, Burning Bright. Play by Peter S. Feibleman. Presented by Oliver Smith and Roger L. Stevens. Associate producers Lyn Austin and Victor Samrock. Booth Theatre, New York, New York. December 22, 1962.

1963 *The Milk Train Doesn't Stop Here Anymore*. Play by Tennessee Williams. Presented by Roger L. Stevens. Associate producers, Lyn Austin and Victor Samrock. Music by Paul Bowles. Morosco Theatre. New York, New York. January 16, 1963.

Andorra. Play by Max Frisch. Presented by Cheryl Crawford and Roger L. Stevens. Biltmore Theatre, New York, New York. February 9, 1963.

Children from Their Games. Play by Irwin Shaw. Produced by Roger L. Stevens and Sam Wanamaker, in association with Lyn Austin and Victor Samrock. Morosco Theatre, New York, New York. April 11, 1963.

Oh Dad, Poor Dad, Mamma's Hung You in the Closet and I'm Feelin' So Sad. Play by Arthur Kopit. Staged by Jerome Robbins. Presented by Roger L. Stevens and T. Edward Hambleton by arrangement with the Phoenix Theatre. Morosco Theatre, New York, New York. August 27, 1963.

Bicycle Ride to Nevada. Play by Robert Thom. Presented by Roger L. Stevens and Herman Shumlin, in association with Nelson Morris and Randolph Hale. Cort Theatre, New York, New York. September 24, 1963.

The Private Ear. The Public Eye. One-act plays by Peter Shaffer. Produced by Roger L. Stevens, in association with Lyn Austin and Victor Samrock, and by arrangement with H. M. Tennent, Ltd. Morosco Theatre, New York, New York. October 9, 1963.

A Case of Libel. Play by Henry Denker. Produced by Roger L. Stevens and Joel Schenker. Longacre Theatre, New York, New York. October 10, 1963.

The Time of the Barracudas. Play by Peter Barnes. Presented by Frederick Brisson, Roger L. Stevens, and Donald Albery. Curran Theatre, San Francisco, California. October 21, 1963.

A Rainy Day in Newark. Play by Howard Teichmann. Produced by Stevens Productions. Belasco Theatre, New York, New York. October 22, 1963.

1964 *The Chinese Prime Minister.* Play by Enid Bagnold. Presented by Roger L. Stevens. Associate producers, Lyn Austin and Victor Samrock. Royale Theatre, New York, New York. January 2, 1964.

Doubletalk. Two one-act plays (*Sarah and the Sax* and *The Dirty Old Man*) by Lewis John Carlino. Presented by Cheryl Crawford and Roger L. Stevens. Theatre de Lys, New York, New York. May 4, 1964.

The Last Analysis. Play by Saul Bellow. Presented by Stevens Productions, Bonfils-Seawell Enterprises, and David Oppenheim. Associate producers, Lyn Austin and Victor Samrock. Belasco Theatre, New York, New York. October 1, 1964.

Beekman Place. Play by Samuel Taylor. Presented by Stevens Productions, Samuel Taylor, Bonfils-Seawell Enterprises. Associate producers, Lyn Austin and Victor Samrock. Morosco Theatre, New York, New York. October 7, 1964.

The Physicists. Play by Friedrich Duerrenmatt. Presented by Allen-Hodgdon, Inc. and Stevens Productions, by arrangement with Robert Whitehead. Martin Beck Theatre, New York, New York. October 13, 1964.

Hang Down Your Head and Die. A musical entertainment devised by David Wright. Presented by Marion Javits by arrangement with Michael Codron, supervised by Stevens Productions, Inc. Mayfair Theatre, New York, New York. October 18, 1964.

Slow Dance on the Killing Ground. Play by William Hanley. Presented by Hume Cronyn, Stevens Productions, Allen-Hodgdon, Inc., and Bonfils-Seawell Enterprises. Plymouth Theatre, New York, New York. November 30, 1964.

Poor Richard. Play by Jean Kerr. Presented by Stevens Productions. Helen Hayes Theatre, New York, New York. December 2, 1964.

1965 *Diamond Orchid.* Play by Jerome Lawrence and Robert E. Lee. Presented by Gilbert Miller in association with Stevens Productions, Inc. Henry Miller's Theatre, New York, New York. February 10, 1965.

Half a Sixpence. Musical based on H. G. Wells's novel, *Kipps*. Book by Beverly Cross. Music and lyrics by David Heneker. Presented by Allen-Hodgdon, Inc., Stevens Productions, Inc., and Harold Fielding. Associate producer, Jane C. Nusbaum. Broadhurst Theatre, New York, New York. April 25, 1965.

The Chinese Prime Minister. Play by Enid Bagnold. Presented by Roger L. Stevens. Globe Theatre, London, UK. May 20, 1965.

The Homecoming. Play by Harold Pinter. Presented by Roger L. Stevens and Peter Hall. Aldwych Theatre, London, UK. June 3, 1965.

1969 *Indians.* Play by Arthur Kopit. Presented by Lyn Austin, Oliver Smith, Joel Schenker, and Roger L. Stevens. Brooks Atkinson Theatre, New York, New York. October 13, 1969.

1970 *Sheep on the Runway*. Play by Art Buchwald. Presented by Roger L. Stevens, Robert Whitehead, and Robert W. Dowling. Helen Hayes Theatre, New York, New York. January 31, 1970.

Conduct Unbecoming. Play by Barry England. Presented by Donald Albery and Roger L. Stevens. Ethel Barrymore Theatre, New York, New York. October 12, 1970.

1971 *Mass*. Music by Leonard Bernstein. Presented by Kennedy Center Productions. Opera House, John F. Kennedy Center for the Performing Arts, Washington, D.C. September 8, 1971.

Old Times. Play by Harold Pinter. Presented by Roger L. Stevens in association with the Royal Shakespeare Company. Billy Rose Theatre, New York, New York. November 16, 1971.

1972 *The Country Girl*. Play by Clifford Odets. Presented by Roger L. Stevens in association with Hugh O'Brien. Billy Rose Theatre, New York, New York. March 15, 1972.

Captain Brassbound's Conversion. Play by George Bernard Shaw. Presented by Roger L. Stevens and Arthur Cantor by arrangement with H. M. Tennent, Ltd. Ethel Barrymore Theatre, New York, New York. April 17, 1972.

Lost in the Stars. Musical by Maxwell Anderson and Kurt Weill. Presented by the Kennedy Center. Imperial Theatre, New York, New York. April 18, 1972.

The Marquise. Play by Noel Coward. Presented by the Kennedy Center and the Triumph Theater. Eisenhower Theatre, John F. Kennedy Center for the Performing Arts, Washington, D.C. May 29, 1972.

The Pleasure of His Company. Play by Samuel Taylor and Cornelia Otis Skinner. Presented by Kennedy Center Productions and Roger L. Stevens. Eisenhower Theatre, John F. Kennedy Center for the Performing Arts, Washington, D.C. July 11, 1972.

The Lincoln Mask. Play by V. J. Longhi. Presented by the Kennedy Center in association with Albert Seldon and Jerome Minskoff. Eisenhower Theatre, John F. Kennedy Center for the Performing Arts, Washington, D.C. September 19, 1972.

The Creation of the World and Other Business. Play by Arthur Miller. Presented by the Kennedy Center and Robert Whitehead. Eisenhower Theatre, John F. Kennedy Center for the Performing Arts, Washington, D.C. October 17, 1972.

1973 *The Jockey Club Stakes*. Play by William Douglas Home. Presented by the Kennedy Center. Cort Theatre, New York, New York. January 24, 1973.

Out Cry. Play by Tennessee Williams. Presented by the Kennedy Center and David Merrick. Eisenhower Theatre, John F. Kennedy Center for the Performing Arts, Washington, D.C. February 5, 1973.

Finishing Touches. Play by Jean Kerr. Presented by Robert Whitehead and Roger L. Stevens. Plymouth Theatre, New York, New York. February 8, 1973.

The Enchanted. Play by Jean Giraudoux. Presented by the Kennedy Center Productions. Eisenhower Theatre, John F. Kennedy Center for the Performing Arts, Washington, D.C. March 2, 1973.

The Blacks. Play by Jean Genet. Presented by the Kennedy Center and the D.C. Black Repertory Company. Eisenhower Theatre, John F. Kennedy Center for the Performing Arts, Washington, D.C. May 26, 1973.

Summer and Smoke. Play by Tennessee Williams. Presented by the Kennedy Center. Eisenhower Theatre, John F. Kennedy Center for the Performing Arts, Washington, D.C. July 17, 1973

The Real Inspector Hound. Play by Tom Stoppard. Presented by Kennedy Center Productions. Eisenhower Theatre, John F. Kennedy Center for the Performing Arts, Washington, D.C. August 9, 1973.

Full Circle. Play by Erich Maria Remarque. Presented by the Kennedy Center Productions. Eisenhower Theatre, John F. Kennedy Center for the Performing Arts, Washington, D.C. October 6, 1973.

The Prodigal Daughter. Play by David Turner. For Kennedy Center Productions by Whitehead/Stevens. Eisenhower Theatre, John F. Kennedy Center for the Performing Arts, Washington, D.C. November 1, 1973.

1974 *The Freedom of the City.* Play by Brian Friel. Presented by the Kennedy Center Productions with Hale Matthews by arrangement with the Goodman Theater Center. Alvin Theatre, New York, New York. February 17, 1974.

Jumpers. Play by Tom Stoppard. Presented for Kennedy Center Productions, Frederick Brisson, and James Nederlander. Billy Rose Theatre, New York, New York. April 22, 1974.

The Headhunters. Play by Henry Denker. Presented by Kennedy Center Productions. Eisenhower Theatre, John F. Kennedy Center for the Performing Arts, Washington, D.C. May 1, 1974.

Perfect Pitch. Play by Samuel Taylor. Presented by the Kennedy Center and Richmond Crinkley. Eisenhower Theatre, John F. Kennedy Center for the Performing Arts, Washington, D.C. June 10, 1974.

Lloyd George Knew My Father. Play by William Douglas Home. Presented by Paul Elliott and Duncan C. Weldon in association with the Kennedy Center. Eisenhower Theatre, John F. Kennedy Center for the Performing Arts, Washington, D.C. July 2, 1974.

London Assurance. Play by Dion Boucicault. Adapted by Ronald Eyre. Presented by James Nederlander, Eddie Kulukundis, and Roger L. Stevens. Palace Theatre, New York, New York. December 5, 1974.

1975 *Present Laughter.* Play by Noel Coward. Presented by Kennedy Center Productions. Eisenhower Theatre, John F. Kennedy Center for the Performing Arts, Washington, D.C. April 29, 1975.

The Scarecrow. Play by Percy MacKaye. Presented by Kennedy Center Productions. Eisenhower Theatre, John F. Kennedy Center for the Performing Arts, Washington, DC. August 10, 1975.

The Skin of Our Teeth. Play by Thornton Wilder. Presented by Ken Marsolais, with the Kennedy Center-Xerox American Bicentennial Theater. Mark Hellinger Theatre, New York, New York. September 9, 1975.

Summer Brave. Play by William Inge. Presented by Barry M. Brown, Burry Fredrik, Fritz Holtz, and Sally Sears, in association with Robert V. Straus in the American Bicentennial Theatre Series. ANTA Theatre, New York, New York. October 26, 1975.

Sweet Bird of Youth. Play by Tennessee Williams. Presented by Michael Harvey, Harvey Frand, and the Kennedy Center-Xerox Corporation American Bicentennial Theatre. Harkness Theatre, New York, New York. December 29, 1975.

The Royal Family. Play by George S. Kaufman and Edna Ferber. Presented by Barry M. Brown, Burry Fredrik, Fritz Holtz, and Sally Sears in the American Bicentennial Theater Series. Helen Hayes Theatre, New York, New York. December 30, 1975.

1976 *A Matter of Gravity.* Play by Enid Bagnold. Presented by Robert Whitehead, Roger Stevens, and Konrad Matthaei. Broadhurst Theatre, New York, New York. February 3, 1976.

The Heiress. Play by Ruth and Augustus Goetz. An American Bicentennial Theatre Production presented by Steven Beckler and Thomas C. Smith. Broadhurst Theatre, New York, New York. April 20, 1976.

1600 Pennsylvania Avenue. Musical by Alan Jay Lerner and Leonard Bernstein. Presented by Roger L. Stevens and Robert Whitehead. Mark Hellinger Theatre, New York, New York. May 4, 1976.

Legend. Play by Samuel Taylor. Presented by Gladys Rackmil and Kennedy Center Productions. Ethel Barrymore Theatre, New York, New York. May 13, 1976.

Rip Van Winkle. Adapted by Joshua Logan and Ralph Allen. Presented by Roger L. Stevens and Richard Crinkley in conjunction with the Xerox Corporation for the Kennedy Center American Bicentennial Theater. Eisenhower Theatre, John F. Kennedy Center for the Performing Arts, Washington, D.C. June 28, 1976.

The Magnificent Yankee. Play by Emmet Lavery. Presented by the Kennedy Center-Xerox Corporation American Bicentennial Theatre. Eisenhower Theatre, John F. Kennedy Center for the Performing Arts, Washington, D.C. June 29, 1976.

A Texas Trilogy. Three plays by Preston Jones: *LuAnn Hampton Lavery Oberlander*, *The Last Meeting of the Knights of the White Magnolias*, and *Oldest Living Graduate*. Presented for the Kennedy Center by Whitehead/Stevens. Broadhurst Theatre, New York, New York. September 21, 1976.

Dirty Linen, New-Found-land. Plays by Tom Stoppard. Presented by the Kennedy Center, Elliot Martin, and InterAction Trust Ltd. Eisenhower Theatre, John F. Kennedy Center for the Performing Arts, Washington, D.C. October 6, 1976.

No Man's Land. Play by Harold Pinter. Presented by Roger L. Stevens and Robert Whitehead in association with Frank Milton. Longacre Theatre, New York, New York. November 9, 1976.

1977 *Travesties*. Play by Tom Stoppard. Presented by the Kennedy Center. Eisenhower Theatre, John F. Kennedy Center for the Performing Arts, Washington, D.C. January 4, 1977.

Annie. Musical. Book by Thomas Meehan. Music by Charles Strouse. Lyrics by Martin Charnin. Presented by Mike Nichols, Irwin Meyer, Stephen R. Friedman, Lewis Allen, Alvin Nederlander Associates, Inc, and Icarus Productions. Alvin Theatre, New York, New York. April 21, 1977.

The Archbishop's Ceiling. Play by Arthur Miller. Presented by Robert Whitehead and Roger L. Stevens. Eisenhower Theatre, John F. Kennedy Center for the Performing Arts, Washington, D.C. April 30, 1977.

The Master Builder. Play by Henrik Ibsen. Presented by the Kennedy Center in association with Connecticut Theatre Foundation, Inc. Eisenhower Theatre, John F. Kennedy Center for the Performing Arts, Washington, D.C. June 1, 1977.

Absent Friends. Play by Alan Ayckbourne. Presented by the Kennedy Center in association with Connecticut Theatre Foundation, Inc. Eisenhower Theatre, John F. Kennedy Center for the Performing Arts, Washington, D.C. July 11, 1977.

Do You Turn Sommersaults. Play by Aleksei Arbuzov. Presented by the Kennedy Center and James Nederlander in association with Cheryl Crawford. Eisenhower Theatre, John F. Kennedy Center for the Performing Arts, Washington, D.C. August 17, 1977.

The Merchant. Play by Arnold Wesker. Presented by the Kennedy Center, the Shubert Organization, Roger Berlind, and Eddie Kulukundis. Eisenhower Theatre, John F. Kennedy Center for the Performing Arts, Washington, D.C. September 28, 1977.

A Touch of the Poet. Play by Eugene O'Neill. Presented by the Kennedy Center and Elliot Martin Productions. Eisenhower Theatre, John F. Kennedy Center for the Performing Arts, Washington, D.C. November 15, 1977.

1978 *Deathtrap*. Play by Ira Levin. Presented by Alfred de Liagre, Jr. and Roger L. Stevens. The Music Box Theatre, New York, New York. February 26, 1978.

The Mighty Gents. Play by Richard Wesley. Presented by James Lipton Productions with the Shubert Organization and Ron Dante. Eisenhower Theatre, John F. Kennedy Center for the Performing Arts, Washington, D.C. March 7, 1978.

Gracious Living. Play by Samuel Taylor. Presented by the Kennedy Center. Eisenhower Theatre, John F. Kennedy Center for the Performing Arts, Washington, D.C. May 3, 1978.

Players. Play by David Williamson. Presented by the Kennedy Center, Eddie Kulukundis, and Backstage Productions. Eisenhower Theatre, John F. Kennedy Center for the Performing Arts, Washington, D.C. July 18, 1978.

The Last of Mrs. Cheyney. Play by Fredrick Lonsdale. Presented by Kennedy Center Productions. Eisenhower Theatre, John F. Kennedy Center for the Performing Arts, Washington, D.C. August 26, 1978.

First Monday in October. Play by Robert E. Lee and Jerome Lawrence. Presented by Kennedy Center Productions, Roger L. Stevens, and Plumstead Theater Society, Inc. Majestic Theatre, New York, New York. October 3, 1978.

Semmelweis. Play by Howard Sackler. Presented for the Kennedy Center by Robert Whitehead. Eisenhower Theatre, John F. Kennedy Center for the Performing Arts, Washington, D.C. October 6, 1978.

Wings. Play by Arthur Kopit. Presented by the Kennedy Center in association with Claus Von Bulow. Eisenhower Theatre, John F. Kennedy Center for the Performing Arts, Washington, D.C. December 26, 1978.

1979 *Bedroom Farce*. Play by Alan Ayckbourn. Presented by Whitehead-Stevens, George W. George, and Frank Milton. Brooks Atkinson Theatre, New York, New York. March 29, 1979.

Carmelina. Musical with book by Joseph Stein and music by Alan Jay Lerner. Presented by Roger L. Stevens, J. W. Fisher, Joan Cullman, and Jujamcyn Productions. St. James Theatre, New York, New York. April 8, 1979.

Comédie Française. The Kennedy Center with the cooperation of L'Association Française pour L'Action Artistique presents *La Puce a l'Oreille*. Play by Georges Feydeau. May 22-24, 1979; Le *Misanthrope*. Play by Moliere May 25-27, 1979. Eisenhower Theatre, John F. Kennedy Center for the Performing Arts, Washington, D.C.

Home and Beauty. Play by W. Somerset Maugham. Presented by the Kennedy Center. Eisenhower Theatre, John F. Kennedy Center for the Performing Arts, Washington, DC. June 1, 1979.

Night and Day. Play by Tom Stoppard. Presented by James M. Nederlander, Kennedy Center Productions, and Michael Codron. ANTA Theatre, New York, New York. November 27, 1979.

1980 *The Art of Dining*. Play by Tina Howe. Presented by the New York Shakespeare Festival, Joseph Papp, and the Kennedy Center. Eisenhower Theatre, John F. Kennedy Center for the Performing Arts, Washington, D.C. January 1, 1980.

Betrayal. Play by Harold Pinter. Presented by Roger Stevens, Robert Whitehead, and James Nederlander. Trafalgar Theatre, New York, New York. January 5, 1980.

Whose Life Is It Anyway? Play by Brian Clark. Nederlander Organization and the Kennedy Center. Eisenhower Theatre, John F. Kennedy Center for the Performing Arts, Washington, D.C. June 20, 1980.

Charlie and Algernon. Musical by David Rogers and Charles Strouse. Presented by the Kennedy Center, Isobel Robins Konecky, the Fisher Theatre Foundation, and the Folger Theatre Group. Eisenhower Theatre, John F. Kennedy Center for the Performing Arts, Washington, D.C. July 31, 1980.

Richard III. Play by William Shakespeare. Presented by the Kennedy Center and the American Shakespeare Theatre. Eisenhower Theatre, John F. Kennedy Center for the Performing Arts, Washington, D.C. September 2, 1980.

Lunch Hour. Play by Jean Kerr. Presented by Robert Whitehead and Roger L. Stevens. Ethel Barrymore Theatre, New York, New York. November 12, 1980.

Mixed Couples. Play by James Prideaux. Presented by the Kennedy Center and Frederick Brisson. Eisenhower Theatre, John F. Kennedy Center for the Performing Arts, Washington, D.C. November 19, 1980.

Hijinks! Musical adapted by Robert Kalfin, Steve Brown, and John McKinney from *Captain Jinx of the Horse Marines*, by Clyde Fitch. Presented by the Chelsea Theater Center, Robert Kalfin, A. Harrison Cromer, the Fisher Theater Foundation, and Roger L. Stevens. Chelsea Theatre Center, Cheryl Crawford Theatre, New York, New York. December 17, 1980.

A Partridge in a Pear Tree. Play by Leslie Stevens. Presented by the Kennedy Center and Empress Productions. Eisenhower Theatre, John F. Kennedy Center for the Performing Arts, Washington, D.C. December 23, 1980.

1981 *Sarah in America*. Play by Ruth Wolff. Presented by Kennedy Center Productions. Eisenhower Theatre, John F. Kennedy Center for the Performing Arts, Washington, D.C. February 4, 1981.

Willie Stark. Opera by Carlisle Floyd. The Kennedy Center and Houston Grand Opera. Opera House, John F. Kennedy Center for the Performing Arts, Washington, D.C. May 9, 1981.

Oh Brother! Musical by Donald Driver and Michael Valenti. Presented by Zev Bufman and the Kennedy Center with the Fisher Theatre Foundation, Joan Cullman, and Sidney Shlenker. Eisenhower Theatre, John F. Kennedy Center for the Performing Arts, Washington, D.C. September 28, 1981.

The West Side Waltz. Play by Ernest Thompson. Presented by Robert Whitehead and Roger L. Stevens in association with the Center Theater Group—Ahmanson. Ethel Barrymore Theatre, New York, New York. November 19, 1981.

The Physicists. Play by Friedrich Duerrenmatt. Presented by the Kennedy Center and the CBS/Broadcast Group. Eisenhower Theatre, John F. Kennedy Center for the Performing Arts, Washington, D.C. December 10, 1981.

1982 *Little Johnny Jones*. Musical by George M. Cohan. Presented by James Nederlander, Steven Leber, David Krebs, and the Kennedy Center. Opera House, John F. Kennedy Center for the Performing Arts, Washington, D.C. January 7, 1982.

The Late Christopher Bean. Play by Sidney Howard. Presented by the Kennedy Center and the CBS/Broadcast Group in association with Martha Scott and James Nederlander. Eisenhower Theatre, John F. Kennedy Center for the Performing Arts, Washington, D.C. January 22, 1982.

Medea. Adapted from Euripides by Robinson Jeffers. Presented by the Kennedy Center in association with the Clarence Brown Company. Eisenhower Theatre, John F. Kennedy Center for the Performing Arts, Washington, D.C. March 3, 1982.

Tartuffe. Adapted from the Molière play by Simon Gray. Presented by the Kennedy Center and the CBS/Broadcast Group. Eisenhower Theatre, John F. Kennedy Center for the Performing Arts, Washington, D.C. April 22, 1982.

The Dining Room. Play by A. R. Gurney, Jr. Presented by the Kennedy Center and the CBS/Broadcast Group in association with Playwrights Horizons, Inc. Eisenhower Theatre, John F. Kennedy Center for the Performing Arts, Washington, D.C. June 3, 1982.

Twice Around the Park. Play by Murray Schisgal. Presented by the Kennedy Center and Peter Witt. Eisenhower Theatre, John F. Kennedy Center for the Performing Arts, Washington, D.C. August 24, 1982 .

Ghosts. Play by Henrik Ibsen. Presented by the Kennedy Center, the CBS/Broadcast Group, and James M. Nederlander. Brooks Atkinson Theatre, New York, New York. August 30, 1982.

Monday After the Miracle. Play by William Gibson. Presented by the Kennedy Center, Raymond Katz, and Sandy Gallin. Eisenhower Theatre, John F. Kennedy Center for the Performing Arts, Washington, D.C. October 8, 1982.

Outrage. Play by Henry Denker. Presented by Kennedy Center Productions. Eisenhower Theatre, John F. Kennedy Center for the Performing Arts, Washington, D.C. December 9, 1982.

1983 *Toyer*. Play by Gardner McKay. Presented by the Kennedy Center, Neil Hartley, Tony Richardson, and George Yaneff. Eisenhower Theatre, John F. Kennedy Center for the Performing Arts, Washington, D.C. January 26, 1983.

You Can't Take It with You. Play by Moss Hart and George S. Kaufman. Presented by the Kennedy Center, Ken Marsolais, Karl Allison, and Bryan Bantry. Eisenhower Theatre, John F. Kennedy Center for the Performing Arts, Washington, D.C. February 22, 1983.

On Your Toes. Musical. Music by Richard Rodgers, book by Lorenz Hart and George Abbott. Presented by Alfred de Liagre, Jr., Roger L. Stevens, John Mauceri, Donald Seawell, and Andre Pastoria. ANTA Theatre, New York, New York. March 6, 1983.

Make and Break. Play by Michael Frayn. Presented by the Kennedy Center Productions. Eisenhower Theatre, John F. Kennedy Center for the Performing Arts, Washington, D.C. April 4, 1983.

Room Service. Play by John Murray and Allen Boretz. Presented by the Kennedy Center. Eisenhower Theatre., John F. Kennedy Center for the Performing Arts, Washington, D.C. May 23, 1983.

Noises Off. Play by Michael Frayn. Presented by James Nederlander, Robert Fryer, Jerome Minskoff, the Kennedy Center, and Michael Codron in association with Jonathan Farkas. Eisenhower Theatre, John F. Kennedy Center for the Performing Arts, Washington, D.C. October 17, 1983.

1984 *End of the World*. Play by Arthur Kopit. Presented by the Kennedy Center and Michael Frazier. Eisenhower Theatre, John F. Kennedy Center for the Performing Arts, Washington, D.C. March 28, 1984.

Death of a Salesman. Play by Arthur Miller. Presented by Robert Whitehead and Roger L. Stevens. Broadhurst Theatre, New York, New York. March 29, 1984.

When Hell Freezes Over, I'll Skate. Musical by Vinnette Carroll. Presented by the Kennedy Center, ANTA, Art Squires in association with Barbara Productions, Anita MacShane, and the Urban Arts Theatre. Eisenhower Theatre, John F. Kennedy Center for the Performing Arts, Washington, D.C. May 2, 1984.

Master Class. Play by David P. Pownall. Presented by the Kennedy Center and Roger L. Stevens. Eisenhower Theatre, John F. Kennedy Center for the Performing Arts, Washington, D.C. September 16, 1984.

1986 *The Petition*. Play by Brian Clarke. Presented by Robert Whitehead and Roger L. Stevens and the Shubert Organization in association with Astramead Ltd. and Freeshooter Productions Ltd. John Golden Theatre, New York, New York. April 24, 1986.

The Caine Mutiny Court-Martial. Play by Herman Wouk. Presented by the Kennedy Center and Joseph Wouk. Eisenhower Theatre, John F. Kennedy Center for the Performing Arts, Washington, D.C. May 28, 1986.

The Perfect Party. Play by A. R. Gurney. Presented by the Kennedy Center. Eisenhower Theatre, John F. Kennedy Center for the Performing Arts, Washington, D.C. December 20, 1986.

1987 *Citizen Tom Paine*. Play by Howard Fast. Presented by the Kennedy Center and ANTA. Eisenhower Theatre, John F. Kennedy Center for the Performing Arts, Washington, D.C. February 27, 1987.

Opera Comique. Play by Nagle Jackson. Presented by the Kennedy Center and ANTA. Eisenhower Theatre, John F. Kennedy Center for the Performing Arts, Washington, D.C. May 2, 1987.

Sherlock's Last Case. Play by Charles Marowitz . Presented by the Kennedy Center, ANTA, Alfie Productions, and the Landmark Entertainment Group. Eisenhower Theatre, John F. Kennedy Center for the Performing Arts, Washington, D.C. June 23, 1987.

I Never Sang for My Father. Play by Robert Anderson. Presented by Jay H. Fuchs, the Kennedy Center, ANTA, and PACE Theatrical Group. Eisenhower Theatre, John F. Kennedy Center for the Performing Arts, Washington, D.C. September 3, 1987.

Breaking the Code. Play by Hugh Whittemore. Presented by the Kennedy Center, ANTA, Jerome Minskoff, Duncan C. Weldon, James Nederlander by arrangement with Triumph Theatre Productions, Ltd., and Michael Redington. Eisenhower Theatre, John F. Kennedy Center for the Performing Arts, Washington, D.C. October 1, 1987.

Contributors

RUTH MAYLEAS's career has encompassed work with major national and international arts funding and service agencies. For a decade in the eighties and early nineties, she directed the Ford Foundation's arts program. From 1966 to 1978 Ms. Mayleas was the first director of the Theatre Program of the National Endowment for the Arts. She is currently a vice-president of the League of Professional Theatre Women and head of its program committee. Ms. Mayleas is also the author of *Theatre Artist's Resource* (Watson-Guptill, 1999), a national guide to advanced training resources and opportunities for theatre artists.

TOM PRIDEAUX (1908-1993) was theatre and amusement editor and later entertainment editor for *Life* magazine. He was a playwright and author of the biography *Love or Nothing: The Life and Times of Ellen Terry* and *World Theater in Pictures: From Ancient Times to Modern Broadway*.

DAVID RICHARDS was a theatre critic for the *Washington Star*, the *Washington Post*, and the *New York Times*. He is the author of *Played Out: The Jean Seberg Story*. He is also the coauthor with Leonard Foglia of *Face Down in the Park* and *One Ragged Ridge Road*. He divides his time between New York and Mexico.

WALTER ZVONCHENKO is the specialist in theatre for the Music Division of the Library of Congress.

ISBN 0-8444-1053-5